Discover...

St. Kit

Columbus' F

Frank Sharman &
Amalia Stone

CREOLE PUBLISHING

Creole Publishing
St. Kitts, West Indies
and Sussex, England.

First published 1987

Published by Creole Publishing
Box 83, St. Kitts, West Indies.
Associated companies in USA & England

CATALOGUE DATA
Authors: Sharman, F./Stone, A.
Title: St. Kitts - Discover - Columbus' Favourite Island.
Subject: St. Kitts - Description and Travel - Guide-books
Publisher: Creole Publishing Company, St. Kitts, West Indies.

ISBN 0-944185-00-2

Printed in Sussex, England, by Creole Design & Print.

Contents

The Editors & Publisher gratefully acknowledge:

Debbie Shamma'a - Researcher, Journalist & Sub-Editor - without whose tremendous contributions, this book would never have made it on time.

Richard 'Rickie' Skerrit - the dynamic Executive Director of the Chamber of Industry & Commerce.

Sir Probyn Innis - former Governor of St. Kitts, Author and distinguished Historian.

Terry Stone - General Manager of SKANTEL (St. Kitts & Nevis Telecommunications Limited).

Evan Blonder & Keith Gold - Senior Students of Veterinary Medicine at St. Kitts' Ross University.

Lloyd Matheson - Historian, Curator & acknowledged 'master' of the history of Brimstone Hill Fortress.

Peter van Hamel - the energetic, problem-solving Managing Director of the St. Kitts' Sugar Industry

Livingstone Jackson - Photographer and Designer, for his perceptive views of our paradise in the sun.

Sandra Goodwin - the noted Marine Photographer, for revealing the beauty of the 'underwater kingdom'.

The Authors respectfully dedicate this book to

'The People of St. Kitts'

- whose friendly smiles welcomed us as 'locals'.

FOREWORD

by Sir Clement Arrindell, CGMC., GCVO., Q.C.
Governor General of St Kitts and Nevis

GOVERNMENT HOUSE.
ST KITTS.
WEST INDIES.

I have often regretted the fact that, despite its undoubted charms, its peaceful character and great natural beauty, Saint Kitts does not boast a colour guidebook to its attractions.

This surprising default at last is being redressed, and I cannot applaud too highly the initiative of the local publishers. This commendable enterprise has put us greatly in their debt. And I must not overlook the many residents whose marvelous contributions have helped in this worthy exercise.

With this enchanting guide as a companion, may you also 'discover St Kitts' and come to know the island that I love so well.

Governor General

Illustration - Stuart Orchard/Dawn Carey

CHAPTER ONE

Discovering St. Kitts - the early visitors

St. Kitts, in the northern Leeward Islands of the Eastern Caribbean, is 1,300 miles southeast of Miami and 200 miles south-east of the island of Puerto Rico. The island is 65 square miles of verdant terrain in the shape of a cricket or baseball bat, with a mountainous central region. The highest peak, Mount Liamuiga, grandly rises out of the clouds at 3,792 feet. Liamuiga, Carib for Fertile Land, was the name given to the island by its earliest Amerindian inhabitants.

Out of the Amazon

Arawak Indians with a 1,400 year history in the Caribbean were the first to walk on St. Kitts' shores. They were a peaceful race who dined on fish, whelk, conch, crab and birds, until shortly before the Europeans arrived. It was then that the Caribs canoed north out of the Amazon jungles of Brazil. The fiercer Caribs were cannibals, who killed or enslaved many Arawaks. Carib warriors often took Arawak women as wives or slaves. This union led to the odd situation of a bi-lingual family, in which the females spoke only Arawak and the warrior and his sons spoke only Carib.

Flying Arrows

Young warriors were taught bravery along with practical survival skills. Jamaican historian Bryan Edwards describes how a newborn Carib male was sprinkled with a few drops of his father's blood to transmit courage from father to son. Small boys quickly learned hunting skills - when their food was hung from trees. Their flying arrows needed to pierce it, before they were permitted to eat.

llustration · Stuart Orchard/Dawn Carey

The popular Frigate Bay Caribbean beach, features golden sands and sparkling blue waters against a backdrop of the 450' high Sir Timothy's Hill.

Necklace of Enemy Teeth

Strong and muscular, the Caribs incised their cheeks and stained the cuts black. They painted black and white rings around their eyes and their bodies crimson. Bones and feathers were pierced through noses and necklaces were made of enemies' teeth.

A Patron Saint

Christopher Columbus spotted St. Kitts on his second voyage to the New World in 1493, naming it St. Christopher after his own patron saint. Early English settlers shortened the name to St. Kitts. To this day, both St. Christopher and St. Kitts remain legal names for the island, 'St. Christopher' normally being favoured for formal use in legal documents and 'St. Kitts' more commonly used in everyday speech. Spain claimed the territory by right of discovery, but thoughts of gold and other riches kept them roaming the region and they did not settle on the island. Other famous visitors to the island, allegedly included the English freebooter Sir Francis Drake and the lordly Sir Walter Raleigh, who is credited with introducing tobacco to Europe.

Early Rock Drawings

By the time the first European settlers arrived on St. Kitts, the Arawaks were nearly exterminated, killed off by disease, the Spaniards and the poison manchineel-dipped arrows of their Indian rivals. The Caribs settled inland, up along the mountain rivers. Chieftain Tegreman ruled over a large settlement, in the hills behind the village of Old Road in what is now called Wingfield. The Amerindian rock drawings in the surrounding ravines, appear to date back to prehistoric times.

All Men Were Equal Once

Not easily conquered, the tough and independent Caribs often preferred death to captivity. Many killed themselves, after being captured in battle, by doggedly ingesting large handfuls of earth rather than lose their freedom. They scorned the Europeans, because they showed deference to their superiors, for the Caribs considered all men were absolutely equal. In spite of their hardy character, the once thriving Carib population was small when the early European settlers arrived on St. Kitts.

The wildly beautiful Atlantic coast of St. Kitts tends to be more sparsely inhabited nowadays, despite facing the cooling ocean breezes of the Trade Winds.

Photo - Livingston Jackson

Photo - Livingston Jackson

The 18-hole Championship Golf Course, at Frigate Bay, offers the golf enthusiast a panorama of waving palm trees, lush greens, sandy bunkers and small lagoons.

Just a Short Voyage

St. Kitts' nearest neighbor, her sister island of Nevis, is to the south - across the 2-mile channel known as The Narrows. The longer voyage, by ferryboat from capital to capital is a 45 minute, 13-mile cruise.

Peek at Other Islands

The Dutch island of St. Eustatius (Statia) lies 6 miles off St. Kitts' northern coast. Dutch Saba can often be seen peeking out from behind Statia. On a clear day, the French islands of St. Martin and St. Barthelmey can be spotted. From a plane above St. Kitts, one can see right across to Antigua on exceptionally clear days - a distance of around 80 miles.

A Different World

St. Kitts can be reached by a number of airlines which offer direct flights from New York, Miami, Puerto Rico, St. Martin and Antigua. After landing at Golden Rock Airport, the traveller will delight in a very different experience from the wintry weather so commonly found 'up north' - a world of warm sultry breezes, brilliant blossoms and fascinating history.

Photo - Cessna Corporation

A smooth and streamlined operation is the keynote, when Captain Bob Hitchins takes to the skies - and the friendly service continues to your destination.

Perhaps the ultimate way to 'discover' any island, is to arrive on your own private plane - and that's precisely the very convenient service offered by Bob Hitchins.

Hopping Caribbean Islands for a Living

Conveniently based on the island, **St. Kitts-Nevis Air Charter Services** (Tel: 465-8332/2722), will whisk you off for a shopping or sightseeing day trip to any nearby island in the Leewards, with all the comfort and convenience of a chauffer driven limousine. Or take you up on one of their increasingly popular 'air-photo' trips around St. Kitts and Nevis - for a true birds-eye view and some stunning aerial snapshots.

A Thirty Year Flight-Plan!

Bob Hitchins and his co-pilot, have notched up over 30 years experience in the art of Caribbean island-hopping. Apart from the sheer convenience of a personal 'walk-on service', the comfort of their luxurious, modern six-seater Cessnas makes flying personal fun again. Fully licensed under both U.K. & U.S. standards and insured at Lloyds of London, Bob Hitchin's neat service give you your 'personal' airline.

CHAPTER TWO

St. Christopher -the 'mother' colony

Often called the "Mother Colony" of the West Indies, St. Kitts was the springboard from which both the English and the French began their colonial conquests of the West Indies. After establishing strongholds on St. Kitts, the English moved on to Nevis, Montserrat and later Antigua. The French gained footholds on the islands of St. Martin, St. Eustatius, St. Barthelemy, Martinique & Guadeloupe.

English Strongholds

The first settlers arrived on January 28, 1623. Thomas Warner, his family and 14 carefully selected Englishmen brought their sailing ship, the 'Marmaduke', to beach at what is now Old Road.

An Easy Place to Defend

Fertile soil and abundant water attracted Warner to St. Kitts, as did his belief that a small island would be easier to defend. Carib Chieftain Tegreman granted the newcomers permission to stay and they began planting corn and tobacco.

Pirates and Galleons

Pirates pursuing early European colonists, brought the first French inhabitants to St. Kitts in 1624. Later, a Captain Urbain de Roissy and a Lieutenant Pierre Belain d'Esnambuc were allowed by the English to disembark at Basseterre after their ship was badly damaged in a battle with a Spanish galleon. Sharing the land was easy to agree to in principle, but, in fact, the French and English fought over the territory for nearly 200 years. A see-saw of capture and recapture continued until St. Kitts was declared entirely British in the 1783 Treaty of Versailles.

Photo - Livingston Jackson

The original Pall Mall Square, now known as Independence Square, features an old-world Fountain fringed by Old Colonial buildings - many with large, cool balconies.

A Bloody Massacre

Conflict then slowly died down and the island remained fully or partly under English colonial control. A dark moment in the island's early history ironically resulted from a show of unity between the two foes in 1626. The massacre of over 2,000 Caribs took place at Stonefort Ravine, now known as Bloody Point. Rumours of a planned Carib attack against the settlers led to this pre-emptive slaughter and the Carib population was virtually wiped out on the island.

Living the Good Life

Prosperity in the late 1600's came with the increasing tobacco trade. Word of the good life in the "New World" spread and by 1648 over 12,000 Europeans were living in the island. Dutch tobacco traders made their home in Sandy Point. Irish indentured servants settled on the northwest end of Basseterre in the neighborhood which is still called Irish Town. Crop production expanded to include cotton, indigo, ginger and sugar, which founded the island's later prosperity.

A Little Sweetener

Sugar, probably first introduced into the region by Portuguese Jews from Brazil, arrived on St. Kitts in the late 1640's and forever changed the island's history. The steady fine weather and fertile soil made Kittitian sugar unsurpassed in quality.

On to America

Labour needs thus increased greatly and in 1670 the first slaves were brought to the island. Vast sugar plantations replaced land plots and many farmers and merchants returned to America and Europe.

A Moving Midnight Ceremony

A Crown Colony since 1877, St. Kitts, in federation with Nevis and Anguilla was declared a state in 1967. The trio remained 'in association' with the United Kingdom, until Anguilla went its own way and the twin-island federated nation of St. Kitts & Nevis was declared totally independent on September 19, 1983 when the Kittitian flag was raised for the first time in a moving midnight ceremony in Warner Park, attended by most of the island's population.

The dramatic palm-fringed, black sand beach at Dieppe Bay, forms the perfect setting for Arthur Leaman's elegant and world famous Golden Lemon Hotel.

Photo - Frank Sharman

Photo - Sandra Goodwin

Wild Deer, Green Vervet Monkeys and a host of other wildlife, are the main inhabitants of the romantically beautiful South East Peninsula.

The proud colours of the St. Kitts & Nevis National Flag.

CHAPTER THREE

Government and People - democratic & cultural diversity

St. Kitts and Nevis became an independent Federal State and member of the Commonwealth on September 19, 1983. There is a system of Cabinet government which is rooted in the British style of Parliamentary democracy. Executive power is vested in Her Majesty the Queen, who is represented, on St. Kitts - by her appointed Governor-General.

Elective Democracy

The St. Kitts-Nevis Federal Parliament consists of the Governor-General and a single chamber National Assembly. This Assembly is comprised of elected members, representing constituencies in both islands.

On a Point of Order, Mister Speaker

Not less than three Senators are also appointed by the Governor-General, on the joint advice of the Prime Minister and the Leader of the Parliamentary Opposition. The National Assembly is presided over by a Speaker, elected by the Assembly.

Adult Votes at 18

General Elections are held at intervals of not more than five years under universal adult sufferage. The voting age was reduced to 18 under the Independence Constitution. At present, elections are contested by three political parties. Usually, the leader of the party which appears most likely to command the support of the majority of the elected Representatives in Parliament is appointed Prime Minister and forms the government.

IMF, FAO, UN - and other important initials

After Independence, St. Kitts and Nevis was admitted to membership of the United Nations and several of its Specialised Agencies - including the World Bank, the International Monetary Fund (IMF), the Food and Agricultural Organization (FAO), and the United Nations Educational Scienific and Cultural Organisation (UNESCO). St. Kitts and Nevis is also a member of several regional organisations, which include the Caribbean Community (CARICOM), the Caribbean Development Bank (CDB) and the Organisation of Eastern Caribbean States (OECS).

Worldwide Diplomacy

The Treaty establishing the OECS was signed in Basseterre, on June 18, 1981. It brought together seven territories into one international organisation. Through the agency of the OECS, St. Kitts and Nevis shares joint diplomatic representation at some overseas missions - but has appointed its own diplomats to the United Nations, the Organisation of American States (OAS) and to the United States.

The Governor General's imposing residence, set amid beautifully terraced and landscaped gardens, is a splendid example of Old Colonial type architecture.

Illustration - Dawn Carey

Photo - Livingston Jackson

Every year, usually starting around 5 am on December 26th, St. Kitts celebrates its colourful Carnival - featuring Street Bands, Carnival Queens and Processions.

His Honour - the Queen's Judge

St. Kitts and Nevis falls within the Jurisdiction of the Supreme Court which consists of a Court of Appeal and a High Court. The Chief Justice is appointed by Her Majesty the Queen and Puisne Judges, one of whom is a resident in St. Kitts-Nevis and the Judicial and Legal Services Commission. Decisions of the Court of Appeal may thus be appealed to the Judicial Committee of the Privy Council in England.

A Perfect Cultural Blending

St. Kitts has a well-earned reputation for welcoming people from other lands and islands. It has evolved into a peaceful and relaxed community - with a firm tradition of harmony between the diverse colours, creeds and religions of people who inhabit the island.

Clowns and Bulls make Carnival

In December St. Kitts stages its Carnival. It is a time of fun and frolic when the traditional melodies of the 'Big Drum' and String Band blend with the rhythms of the Steel Bands. The Masquerades, Clowns and the Bull are an inherent part of the national folklore.

Carnival is for the people - all of them
J'ouvert Morning - usually the second day after the official opening of Carnival Week on Christmas Eve, tends to start 'waking up' the town centre, at a very early hour. Traditionally, the first of the many local bands and groups hit the streets at about 5 am - to attract supporters for their all-day 'jamming'.

'Leh we go jammin' - duhn de Bay Front'
The West Indian term 'jammin', means to dance in the streets, usually following a Brass, String or Steel band, that parades slowly round the town on the back of a truck. Each group specially features the carnival's most catchy new musical tune, composed by local calypsonians or by the bands themselves.

Everybody loves the Road March
Popular choice, in the number of followers each Band can collect along the way, usually determines which composition will become the elected 'Road March' carnival hit. The 'winners' attract huge followings, literally jamming the streets from side to side, in the day long revelry, which is the highspot of the Carnival.

The brightly painted boats of the St. Kitts' fishermen, make a delightful and much photographed addition to the palm lined beaches around the island's shores.

Photo - Frank Sharman

Photo - Livingston Jackson

Skilled technicians from The Cable, regularly monitor the Satellite Dish alignment, to ensure that islanders and visitors enjoy a consistently high quality TV reception.

Cable Television makes a Debut in St. Kitts
Strange as it may seem for such a tiny island, St. Kitts residents - and many of the island's hotel - enjoy the benefits of a very modern Cable Television system.

Twelve Channels to Paradise
A group of Dallas-based businessmen, led by Texan entrepreneur Jim Frehner, started **The Cable** as a joint venture with the St. Kitts government. Islanders on the virtually nation-wide network, can simply call The Cable's head office in Central Street (Tel: 465-2588/2233) and get hooked up in a day or so.

Top Quality Colour Entertainment
The Cable's subscribers enjoy the very latest world news from CNN, a tremendous choice of first run movies, educational, business improvement and stunningly filmed Channel 4 Nature documentaries.

Keep In Touch with Home Events
Go-ahead hotels, like the Ocean Terrace Inn and the Sun 'N Sand Beach Village, quickly realised the benefit to guests - and added Cable TV to their attractions.

St. Kitts and Nevis Telecommunications, known locally as SKANTEL, was formed in 1985 as a joint venture between the Government of St. Kitts and Nevis and Cable & Wireless to own and operate the nation's telecommunications system.

A World 'First' in State of the Art

Following up this initiative in a very practical way, SKANTEL embarked on a development programme to modernise the country's telecommunications system and make St. Kitts and Nevis one of the first nations in the world to boast a fully digital telecommunications network - both national and international. SKANTEL employs state of the art technology in Digital Cables, Digital Exchanges, Optical Fibres & Microwave Links.

Telling the World about Paradise

SKANTEL provides services for locals & visitors alike, both at its Basseterre office and at all major hotels. In St. Kitts, you can make international calls, call collect or to the USA, via the handy SKANTEL/ATT 'USA Direct' service. So to make your stay in our island paradise complete, call home - and tell them about it!

Futuristic-looking, high technology circuit boards - control the island's modern telecommunications - currently one of the world's finest systems.

Photo - Len Dance Associates

CHAPTER FOUR

The Town of Basseterre - traditional tranquility

The treaty of May 13, 1627 ceded the town of Basseterre (which means 'leeward' in French nautical terms), and the surrounding lowlands to the French. Later, the English regained control of the whole island but the French name of Basseterre still survives today.

Let's go to The Circus

Over the years Basseterre has suffered its share of disasters, fire, flood and hurricane. The old town of Basseterre was destroyed by fire in 1867. The whole town was burned down and rebuilt, giving way to much wider roads and construction of The Circus.

Always Tomorrow...

The town of Basseterre is "traditional and tranquil" but beautiful in its sleepy and peaceful way. You feel that time has stopped or at least there is no need to rush around... there is always tomorrow!

A Virtually Crime-Free Town

In all that tranquility, there is still the heart of a busy commercial town. And as you tour our quiet and quaint, almost crime-free town - please don't miss our many fascinating places of interest.

Slaves, Witches and Councillors

In 1790, Pall Mall Square was erected for conducting Council Meetings and Slave Auctions. Since the 1983 Independence of St. Kitts and Nevis it has been renamed Independence Square. Popular folklore maintains that the Fountain was used to "dip" the folks who engaged in witchcraft. Around the Square you will still find many charmingly preserved examples of the original Old Colonial style houses.

Photo - Frank Sharman

Charming examples of Old Colonial architecture, many with balconies featuring the decorative wooden 'gingerbread' lattice work, line North Square Street.

Gingerbread and High Finance

The town has kept its old colonial look and most of the houses seen today are the original. Even if they have been repaired, all the work is usually done within the traditional look, as you can see in the local 'gingerbread', which is a type of carved wood and lattice work that adorns many a balcony. You will enjoy wandering around our many picturesque streets where you can see and 'feel' the Old Colonial style of the past, blending gently with the present as the town moves steadily through the 20th century. In the past few years, many new shops and offices have opened in older buildings and maintained the Old Colonial look.

Folk Tales and Legends

The Circus was built in traditional English style, on the pattern of London's famous Piccadilly Circus and is in the heart of the town. Surrounded by the Treasury Building, the 17th century Pretoria Gardens, Barclays Bank, the Royal Bank of Canada and the commercial centre. It is at the Circus that you will find the main taxi rank. Our island taxi drivers are our unofficial "island guides" and always ready to praise the island.

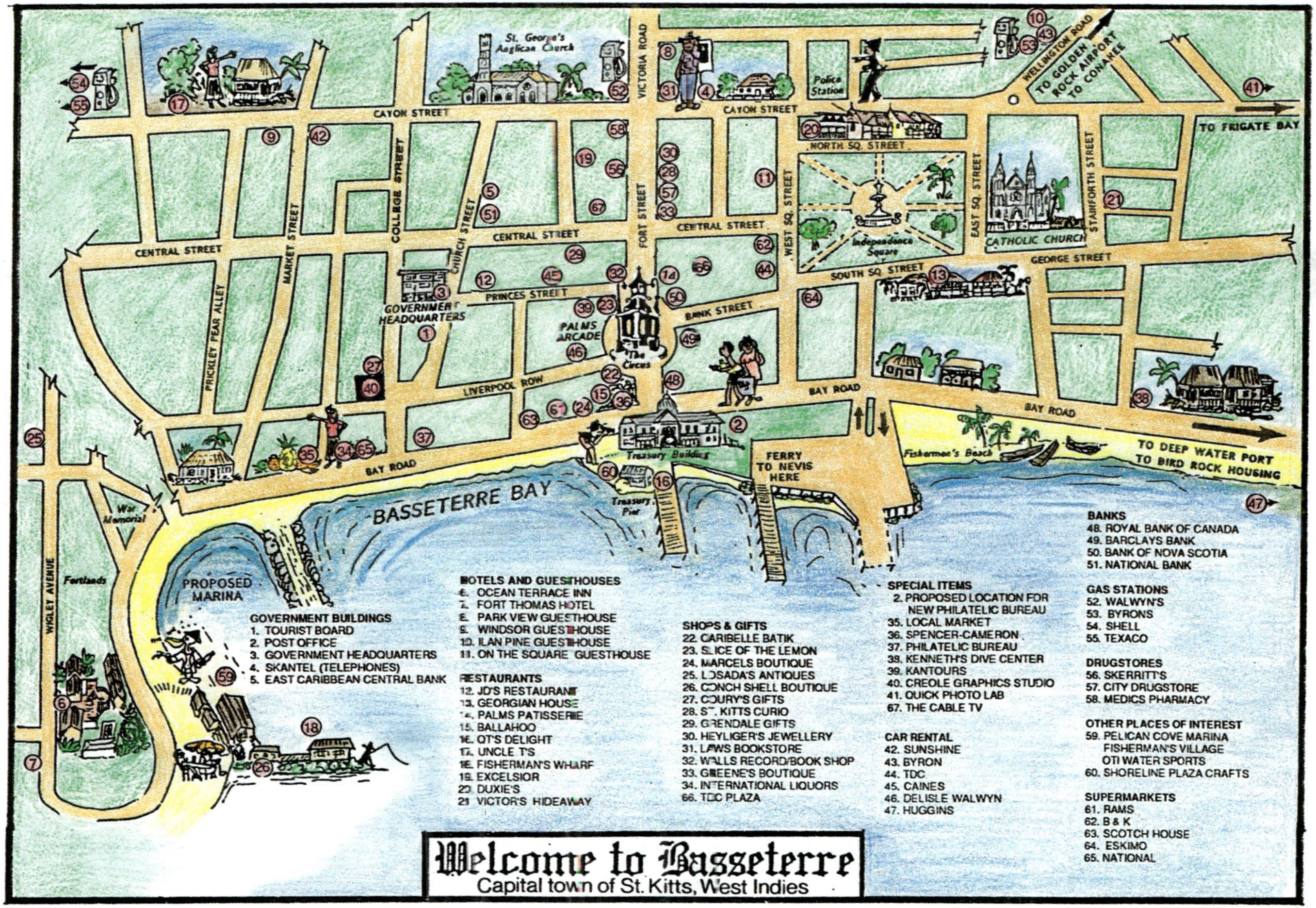

Welcome to Basseterre
Capital town of St. Kitts, West Indies
GOVERNMENT BUILDINGS
1. TOURIST BOARD
2. POST OFFICE
3. GOVERNMENT HEADQUARTERS
4. SKANTEL (TELEPHONES)
5. EAST CARIBBEAN CENTRAL BANK
HOTELS AND GUESTHOUSES
6. OCEAN TERRACE INN
7. FORT THOMAS HOTEL
8. PARK VIEW GUESTHOUSE
9. WINDSOR GUESTHOUSE
10. ILAN PINE GUESTHOUSE
11. ON THE SQUARE GUESTHOUSE
RESTAURANTS
12. JD'S RESTAURANT
13. GEORGIAN HOUSE
14. PALMS PATISSERIE
15. BALLAHOO
16. OT'S DELIGHT
17. UNCLE T'S
18. FISHERMAN'S WHARF
19. EXCELSIOR
20. DUXIE'S
21. VICTOR'S HIDEAWAY
SHOPS & GIFTS
22. CARIBELLE BATIK
23. SLICE OF THE LEMON
24. MARCELS BOUTIQUE
25. LOSADA'S ANTIQUES
26. CONCH SHELL BOUTIQUE
27. COURY'S GIFTS
28. ST. KITTS CURIO
29. GRENDALE GIFTS
30. HEYLIGER'S JEWELLERY
31. LAWS BOOKSTORE
32. WALLS RECORD/BOOK SHOP
33. GREENE'S BOUTIQUE
34. INTERNATIONAL LIQUORS
66. TDC PLAZA
SPECIAL ITEMS
2. PROPOSED LOCATION FOR NEW PHILATELIC BUREAU
35. LOCAL MARKET
36. SPENCER-CAMERON
37. PHILATELIC BUREAU
38. KENNETH'S DIVE CENTER
39. KANTOURS
40. CREOLE GRAPHICS STUDIO
41. QUICK PHOTO LAB
67. THE CABLE TV
CAR RENTAL
42. SUNSHINE
43. BYRON
44. TDC
45. CAINES
46. DELISLE WALWYN
47. HUGGINS
BANKS
48. ROYAL BANK OF CANADA
49. BARCLAYS BANK
50. BANK OF NOVA SCOTIA
51. NATIONAL BANK
GAS STATIONS
52. WALWYN'S
53. BYRONS
54. SHELL
55. TEXACO
DRUGSTORES
56. SKERRITT'S
57. CITY DRUGSTORE
58. MEDICS PHARMACY
OTHER PLACES OF INTEREST
59. PELICAN COVE MARINA
FISHERMAN'S VILLAGE
OTI WATER SPORTS
60. SHORELINE PLAZA CRAFTS
SUPERMARKETS
61. RAMS
62. B & K
63. SCOTCH HOUSE
64. ESKIMO
65. NATIONAL
St. George's Anglican Church
CAYON STREET
VICTORIA ROAD
Police Station
WELLINGTON ROAD
TO GOLDEN ROCK AIRPORT
TO CONAREE
TO FRIGATE BAY
NORTH SQ. STREET
COLLEGE STREET
CHURCH STREET
MARKET STREET
CENTRAL STREET
FORT STREET
WEST SQ. STREET
EAST SQ. STREET
STAINFORTH STREET
Independence Square
CATHOLIC CHURCH
GEORGE STREET
SOUTH SQ. STREET
PRINCES STREET
BANK STREET
GOVERNMENT HEADQUARTERS
PALMS ARCADE
The Circus
PRICKLEY PEAR ALLEY
LIVERPOOL ROW
BAY ROAD
Treasury Building
FERRY TO NEVIS HERE
Fishermen's Beach
TO DEEP WATER PORT
TO BIRD ROCK HOUSING
Treasury Pier
BASSETERRE BAY
War Memorial
Fortlands
WIGLEY AVENUE
PROPOSED MARINA

What's the Time?

The Berkeley Memorial Drinking Fountain and Public Clock are now the focal point of The Circus. It honours Thomas Berkeley, a former President of the General Legislative Council of the Leeward Islands. The St. Kitts Treasury Building is located on the Bay Front in the town centre. Its foundations were first laid in 1891 and it was finally completed in 1894. The building dominates the waterfront and can be seen from miles away by sailors, heading for the modern container terminal and Deep Water Harbour.

A House on Wheels!

One of the most incredible sights you can witness in our island, is the move of a "chattel" house. So called because when the family moves, they do not just move from one house to another, but also move their house, with all its "goods and chattels" (belongings). So if you see a house on the back of a tractor or lorry, do not worry, your eyes are not deceiving you. It is probably just an island family moving from one village to another with all their possessions intact.

Fort Street and the Circus, in the tranquil city of Basseterre, which nestles between the calm Caribbean Sea and the soft green peaks of Monkey and Canada Hills.

Photo - Livingston Jackson

Illustration - Spencer Cameron Gallery

Moving one's residence in St. Kitts, is taken quite literally on many occasions - and one can often see this colourful event as a family's 'chattel house' is moved.

See Our Miniature Art Gallery

The busy and friendly St. Kitts Philatelic Bureau is located on the waterfront, on the Bay Road. A paradise for the serious stamp collector and casual visitor alike.

Limin' by the Bay

In 1880 Basseterre was flooded and the Bay Road's ancient 11/2 mile promenade was destroyed. Since 1890, when major reconstruction took place, it remains as it is today. In earlier times however, there was a sea wall with plants and benches, where people would go to "lime: i.e. just sit around and "see the world go by". Sad as it is, the Bay Road never quite regained its former splendour as the town promenade.

At the End of the Road

The nearby waterfront War Memorial was erected to commemorate the men of the Islands who died in both World Wars. The Memorial was originally located at the eastern side of the Treasury Building, but was moved in the 1950's to its present site at the end of the Bay Road. A memorial service is still held annually with a 2-minute silence to honour the fallen soldiers.

On the Stroke of Midnight...
Warner Park, the local residents' main recreation area and situated in the heart of town, was opened on January 5, 1928 and since then it has seen many exciting cricket matches, fetes and festivals. Site of most of the annual pre-Carnival competitions, it has also been the venue for many official celebration - such as the announcement of Independence, at midnight on September19, 1983 - and for official ceremonies, such as Queen Elizabeth and Prince Phillip's visit in 1985. This also seems to be the favourite place where people congregate, when there is something special to do - like watch a vital local Cricket Match!

Basseterre "Nets" Two Neighbours
Along the Bay Front you will find New Town and Irish Town, these two picturesque original fishing villages, one at each side of Basseterre, now sandwich the commercial heart of Basseterre. Very early in the morning you can often see the colourful local boats and the fishermen leave in search of the daily catch, which they trade straight from their boats as they land. You can't get better or fresher fish than that!

Rosie Cameron-Smith's fine range of Limited Edition lithographic prints, superbly capture the rich texture of many facets of rural life around the island's villages.

Illustration - Spencer Cameron Gallery

CHAPTER FIVE

Trade and Industry - a changing scene

Basseterre is slowly being transformed into a busy business centre. The 20,000 population town has always been the commercial heart of this tiny Caribbean paradise, but, except for a few days each year during Carnival celebrations, has never been described as 'bustling'.

Business is Bustling Every Day
However, with the main Sea Port sitting on its south shore and Golden Rock Airport just five minutes to the north, the movement of an expanding volume of goods and people to and from the island is turning Basseterre into a truly bustling business town.

Valuable Vacationing Visitors
The annual rate of increase of visitors to St. Kitts has averaged in the region of 20 percent for the period 1984-1986. A combined total of approximately 80,000 overnight and yacht/cruise ship visitors arrived in St. Kitts in 1986 and this figure should pass the 100,000 mark in 1988. For an island with a population of less than 40,000, that number of visitors is a very significant factor in the economy.

Structural Improvements
This upsurge in visitor arrivals is helping to change the economic structure of the island and having a valuable, visible impact on Basseterre. The physical requirements for meeting the needs of an expanding population include improved transport, shopping, accomodation and recreational facilities and Basseterre, together with the rest of the island, is transforming to meet the new demands, with private and public construction on the upturn.

A Touch of Sweetness

Because of the small size of the domestic market, St. Kitts manufacturing has always been export oriented. Sugar still remains the largest single export and accounts for about 60 percent of total exports and over 25% of total employment. In recent years, the industry has experienced some difficulties, mainly from a steady fall in world demand and prices. Between 1979 and 1983, the sugar industry's contribution to GDP fell. This has resulted in a new emphasis on non-sugar local manufacturing, the extent of which will startle even the casual observer.

Bits, Bytes and Blouses

There is now over 200,000 square feet of factory space occupied in St. Kitts by both local and foreign-owned companies who are in the business of producing finished or semi-finished products for the neighbouring Caribbean and U.S. markets. About 800 people devote their time daily to producing high quality electronic components such as transformers, PC boards, stators and rotors for the U.S. computer, telecommunications and aerospace industries.

The island's picturesque Deep Water Port on the outskirts of Basseterre, is a safe haven for the many visiting Cruise Ships and all types of commercial shipping.

Photo - Livingston Jackson

Photo - Livingston Jackson

Swaying palms and green lawns, characterise much of Basseterre's light industrial section and offer delightful surroundings for the industrious local work force.

Busy Factories employing Busy People

Another 1,000 people are busy stitching and packaging all types of garments to send around the Caribbean and to North America every week. Other factories are producing food products, furniture and other items, for the domestic market and for export.

New York City - Beware!

St. Kitts produces about 30 percent of domestic food requirements today. An expanding tourism economy provides both a challenge and an opportunity to farmers to produce even more food at more attractive prices. Food imports continue to rise at an alarming rate with the dollar value having doubled in the past 10 years, but this trend is not reflected totally in the sectors of fruits and vegetables, fresh fish and dairy products and eggs where local production is now increasing. St. Kitts today is in the midst of a vital economic diversification which emphasizes the promotion of tourism and the expansion of non-sugar agriculture such as livestock and fisheries. Basseterre will never be New York City, but it won't be long before it can be described as bustling Basseterre.

The firm of **Smiths Gore** (Tel; 465-4100), located near the heart of town on Cayon Street - is St. Kitts' only fully professional and internationally qualified Real Estate Agents and Valuers. They handle Sales and Rentals of all types of land, homes and condominiums and are, in addition, Project Managers, Development Consultants, Valuers and Appraisers.

150 Years of links with the UK, USA and Canada

The local office is associated with Smiths Gore of the UK, which was first established in1840 and with other offices in Tortola, the USA and the Far East. Under the direction of Michael Bentley, with his 25 years of professional real estate experience in the UK, Canada, the USA and the Caribbean, Smiths Gore specialises in sales and rentals, many major project management schemes and development-consulting for a variety of local island and international clients.

A Sister in Tortola

Smiths Gore's sister office in Tortola has been established for over 20 years, and serves a variety of clients throughout the B.V.I. and the region.

The 18th Century look of the building housing the Smiths Gore offices, belies the smooth efficiency of the island's only qualified & professional Real Estate Agents.

Illustration - Dawn Carey

CHAPTER SIX

Let's Go Exploring - discover island secrets

There is plenty to do in St. Kitts, activities for all tastes and most sports are available. Deep-sea fishing, gambling, a visit to an old manor house, a hike to the volcano - just select the pace that suits you. Of course for those that just want to soak up the Caribbean sun, there is plenty of that, too.

A Sense of Wonder Every Day

SCUBA diving must be among the world's most exciting sports and our waters and reefs provide a great variety of sites, in shallow waters for beginners and, in deeper waters, for the more experienced. All that marine life waiting there to be discovered and experienced. Corals, sea feathers, sponges and fans, just for you to enjoy. To see so much marine life - at close range - is a great feeling, which is never lost, either by the beginner or the experienced diver.

Old Wife and the Royals

Among the fish species that are most commonly seen in our waters are: the Parrotfish with its beautiful colours of yellow, red, blue and green, the Pufferfish, Triggerfish (known locally as the 'Old Wife'), Boxfishes of various sizes and Spots (called 'Shellfish' here), Banded Butterflyfish, Squirrelfish, Trumpetfish, Queen Angelfish, Blackbar Soldierfish, Spotfin Butterflyfish, French Angelfish, Royal Gramma, Schoolmaster Snapper and Yellowtail Snapper to name but a few. And of course there are the Barracuda and Spiny Lobster. Very exotic shells are not easily found, but Conch shells are plentiful, and sought for their lovely colours. Few other really large or truly exotic shells are about and the discovery of such a find is indeed a great cause for a celebration.

Take Some Film and Don't Forget the Water
St. Kitts is an ideal place for nature lovers who may like to capture the island's magnificent views on film. What better way to see all those places inaccessible by car than by taking a walk? Remember to wear very comfortable clothing, a hat and sunscreen. Always take plenty of water with you, since in some of the remoter areas you may not find another human being.

Take a Trip - take a Guide
Always be accompanied by someone who knows the area and get an early morning start, before the sun is too high. Unless you have arranged a pickup, please don't forget to reserve some energy for the walk back!

In the Footsteps of Sir Timothy Thornhill
Some of the better known local walks include the trip over Timothy Hill (named after the intrepid English Officer, who marched troops over the hill by night, to surprise the French defenders of Basseterre) to lovely Friar's Beach, the walk down the Southeast Peninsula to Banana Bay (or just part of the way to White House Bay) and the hike to Ottley's Level in the mountains.

The underwater fairy-tale castles, created by Montastrea annularis (commonly called Star Coral), enhance the hidden beauties of St. Kitts' many coral reefs.

Photo - Sandra Goodwin

Photo - Frank Sharman

A short hike to the 450' peak of Sir Timothy's Hill in Frigate Bay, rewards intrepid visitors with a cooling breeze and a spectacular view of the South East Peninsula.

Side Tracking and Other Trips

Once in St. Kitts you can't leave without paying a visit to our sister island of Nevis. You can get there by ferry, check times down at the pier, as the schedule varies daily. LIAT offers daily 5-minute flights across the Channel. If you prefer to follow your own schedule - just charter a boat or even a private plane!

Celebrated Vows for an Admiral

While in Nevis, rent a car or take an island tour with one of the friendly taxi drivers. Be sure to visit the Fig Tree Church where Admiral Horatio Nelson (then a mere Captain) married local Nevisian Fanny Nisbett.

Good for what Ails You - So They Say

Another place of interest is the Bath Hotel, built in 1778. Enjoy a dip in the sulphur spring waters - it is alleged to cure various ills and ailments of all kinds.

Throwing Pots

At Newcastle Pottery, watch the craft creation of hand made pots and other clay items, using the island of Nevis' own famous red clay. They make ideal gifts, too.

To the casual visitor, **Romney Manor and Gardens,** at Old Road, are like a paradise found. Nestling 600 feet above sea level on the slopes of a volcano, the approach through a tropical rain forest and past prehistoric rock drawings climaxes in a riot of colour, which are the beautifully tended and magnificently laid out five acres of the Manor's gardens.

A Photographer's Dream Come True
Majestic lawns, exquisite stonework, a historic Bell Tower, the region's largest tree and a bewildering variety of Birds, Lizards, tropical Flowers, Trees and Shrubs - make Romney Manor (Tel: 465-6253) and its gardens, a photographer's dream, where every shot is sure to capture a new and captivating scene.

And... there's Still More to See!
In addition to the Gardens, with a chance to spot the shy Green Vervet Monkeys, Romney Manor has the most splendid views of Brimstone Hill and beyond. Frequently described as 'the world's most beautiful factory' - you can enjoy watching the artists creating the fabulous and colourful Caribelle Batik fashions.

Romney Manor, a positive jewel of a mansion, is set peacefully amid colourful gardens, ablaze with tropical flowers and rated amongst the Caribbean's finest.

Photo - Caribelle Batik

Photo - Caribelle Batik

Most artists use a pen, pencil, brush or crayon. The creators of Caribelle's lovely batiks, however, use a 'tjanting' tool, hot wax - and a 2,000 year-old technique.

Situated at **Romney Manor** (Tel: 465-6253) is 'the World's Most Beautiful Factory'. Caribelle Batik have made this their home - and are using a 2,000 year old tradition of craftsmanship to produce the world famous, high quality Batik fashions and wallhangings, which are now synonymous with St. Kitts.

Crowned in Batik by Royalty

With a reputation for quality and style, that has spread far beyond this region, Caribelle Batik items have been acquired by Queens, Princesses, Premiers and other world leaders. And by the thousands of delighted visitors who have visited the Manor to watch them carry out the ancient craft of creating fine 'batik'.

See the Quality for Yourself

In a completely open 'workshop', batik is designed and created before your eyes, using pure silks and 100% long staple cotton. Skilled craft workers are delighted to demonstrate, explain or pose for photographs as they work. They also sell their colorful batik items, which are in complete harmony with the 'excitement and colour' of the Caribbean.

With the verdant flora and unique fauna of the tropical rain forests of St. Kitts, you are sure to be left awestruck by this 'close encounter of a natural kind'. **Greg's Rain Forest Tour** (Tel: 465-4121/4122) takes you through a time warp of ancient sugar plantations, then on up to the spectacular scenery of the forests, alive with Old World monkeys and beautiful birds. To explore our rain forests, gives you the pleasure of knowing a truly tropical paradise.

Professional Experience
Try this unforgettable adventure with Greg, whose Kittitian background and years of hotel tour experience will definitely leave you satisfied.

A Popular Tour
A travel journalist recently wrote - 'Greg Pereira leads an absolutely delightful and informative four-hour, late afternoon tour through the canefields up into one of the most spectacular greenbelts in the Caribbean. Greg is a real encyclopedia of the flora and fauna you'll encounter, and shares some compelling overlooks. His volcano tour is more demanding but more compelling'.

Keen amateur naturalist Greg Pereira of the Ocean Terrace Inn, delights in showing off the many undiscovered beauty spots of the island's peaks and tropical interior.

Photo- Greg Pereira

Photo - Sandra Goodwin

Hordes of brightly coloured tropical fish, greet SCUBA divers introduced to the underwater splendour by Kenneth Samuel, St. Kitts' leading PADI Divemaster.

For fun both atop and under the azure waters of St. Kitts, try the Frigate Bay Caribbean beach. There, both **Kenneth's Dive Centre** and **Roy Gumbs Watersports,** help you begin your Caribbean Sea adventures.

Meet a Kittitian Monkey
Located near the Kittitian Monkey Beach Bar, Roy offers Windsurfers, Sunfish, water-skiing and Hobycats. Here is also where you book an afternoon boat trip to the nearby but secluded Friar's Beach.

Discover our Underwater Kingdom
Kenneth's Dive Centre is the place to seek your underwater delights. Kenneth Samuel, a P.A.D.I. Divemaster, offers both Snorkeling and SCUBA diving for qualified divers, as well as a resort course for novices. For 'certified divers', Kenneth's Boat Dives are even more exciting, since he knows the best reefs.

Sunset Cruises with a Lady
Landlubbers can watch the sun go down on Kenneth's 38-foot catamaran, the **'Lady Peggy'**. Reach Kenneth (direct) at 465-2670/8050 - and Roy at 465-8050.

Photo - Frank Sharman

The romance of the Caribbean comes to the fore, as the sun sets over the sparkling blue waters and dramatises the majestic coconut palms of St. Kitts countryside

Photo - Kriss Tours

The fascinating fauna of the island's exotic Rain Forest, never fails to captivate the visitor who ventures on one of Kriss Berry's very popular hiking expeditions.

Discover the secret rain forests of St. Kitts on a unique and unforgettable **Kriss Tours** trip with Vandell "Kriss" Berry (Tel: 465-4042) With 12 years experience as a forest and volcano tour guide, Kriss has much to offer visitors, aside from his knowledge of the trail. Along the way he points out splendid plants, an occasional monkey and he even has a tame Mongoose that often shares the picnic table, once you are atop the Peak.

A Trail of Roots and Vines

A visit to the dormant volcano must surely be one of the most spectacular trips to be made in St. Kitts. The hike to the rim of the Crater takes about 2 hours, including frequent rest-stops to admire points of interest along the way. The final part of the adventure is a 700-foot descent down into the Crater, using a trail studded with roots and vines. Guests who prefer may relax on the rim, instead of making the descent.

The Reclusive Lawyer's Cave

Kriss also offers a shorter trip to Lawyer Stevens' cave. This tour appeals especially to those guests who may find the full day Rain Forest hike a little too arduous.

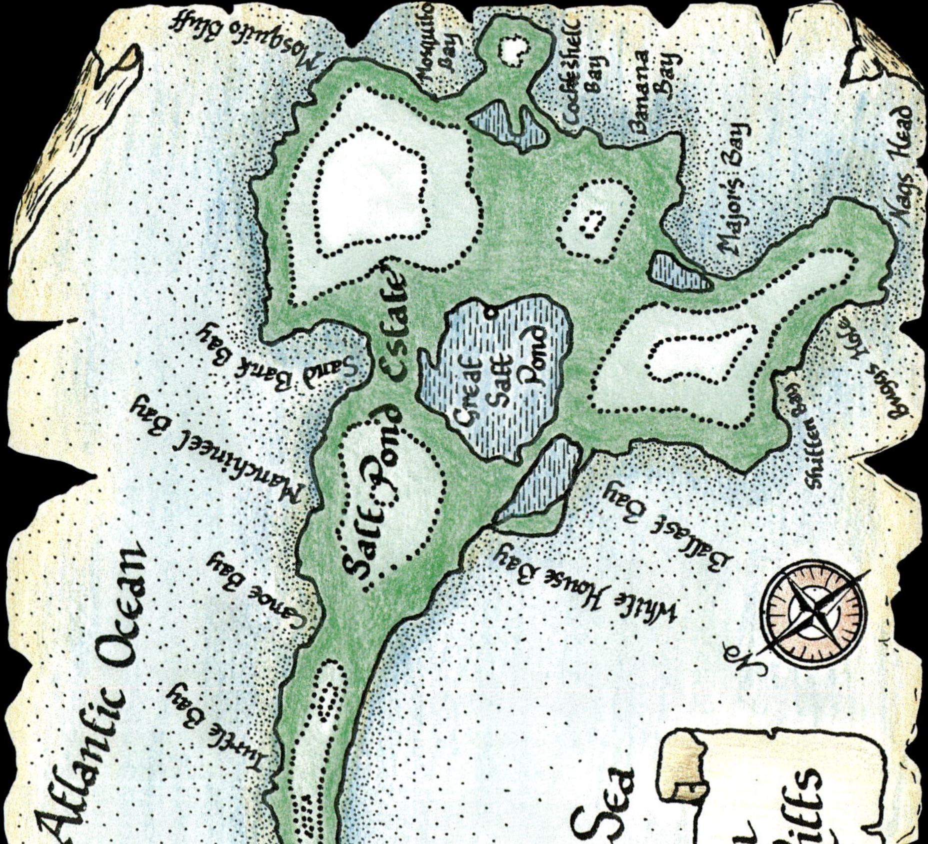

Illustration - Stuart Orchard/Dawn Carey

Exploration, of specific subjects, can lead to a very interesting career - as many young North Americans have discovered on the island of St. Kitts.

Fauna - in Great Detail - for a Career

Reacting to the increasing demand in the USA for fully qualified Veterinarians, **Ross University** (Tel: 465-4161), set up a comprehensively equipped new Veterinary University, besidc thc sparkling blue Caribbean waters, near the island's West Farm Estate.

Hard Work under the Palms of St. Kitts

Life for the Ross students (like all serious students), is not however, an endless round of pleasure under the waving palms. Much hard work and dedicated study are needed to pass the many exams, which are based on the rigorous North American Veterinary standards.

Community Integration at its Best

However, in between studies, most Ross University students still, somehow, find a little time to study the island and its people - and have made many valuable contributions to the rich texture of this island's life.

Discovering the secrets of the animal world, helps to establish many rewarding veterinary careers for the hard-working students at this island learning centre.

Photo - Livingston Jackson

A quick phone call to **Tropical Tours** (Tel: 465-4167/4039), will get you a full day of adventure - cruising the sparkling blue Caribbean - aboard the giant 52 foot long x 26 foot wide **CELICA III Party & Cruise Catamaran,** with a door-to-door service from your hotel to a 'high seas adventure day' and back.

Party like a Pirate

Celica III's deck is the daily scene for all-day Party Cruises that feature such truly piratical activities as Limbo Dancing (with free lessons from the agile crew) - all to the exciting throbbing beat of true Caribbean Reggae and Calypso music, with the Celica's generous Open Bar, topping everyone up on Celica's famous Rum Punch & other free drinks - a service that is freely available all day - so please don't fall overboard!!

Barbecues and Bars of Gold

Plenty of swimming and a spot of snorkeling (there's lots of free equipment aboard), leads you to a delicious Barbecue lunch on a secluded beach. Afterwards, you can try your hand at locating some of the many hoards of Pirate Gold, reputedly hidden all over this region.

A relaxing day cruise, aboard Celica III, one of the island's spacious catamarans, is a memorable experience - and a unique chance to make new friends.

Photo - Leroy Willett

CHAPTER SEVEN

The Sugar Island - centuries of sweetness

When Sir Thomas Warner first landed, Carib Indians were already cultivating small plots of sugar cane, grown mainly for chewing and for producing a crude but potent fermented beverage similar to a sweet beer.

The Sugar Fortunes Begin to Grow

In 1625 on his return, Sir Thomas brought European settlers, determined to make their fortunes in the colonies. At about this period, there was a new demand for sugar in Europe and the settlers found that sugar cane grew extremely well on the island. Sugar soon became the main crop, yielding high profits. Thus began the expansion of cane production.

Picturesque Old Stone Mills

Sugar 'factories' sprang up on every estate, powered by massively built stone and wooden windmills. Built on slopes, to catch the Trade Winds, these mills were the work centre of the Estate Yard. Great Houses, built to catch the same cooling winds - feature large balconies overlooking what are often now mere ruins. Today, over 44 of these picturesque old mills can be seen, dotted around the island - some superbly converted.

Cargos of Trinkets and Cloth

The early history of sugar, was also the early history of slavery. Slaves were bought from Africa, usually sold to the slavers by rival tribesmen. The slave-traders often carried cargos of cloth and gaudy trinkets to barter for slaves, who were then transported to the Caribbean. Re-loaded with spices and sugar, the ships returned to Europe to buy more cloth and trinkets - and sail for Africa again. This shameful practice lasted for many years - until slavery & the slave trade were abolished.

Sail Gives Way to Steam

In 1911, Henckell Du Buisson & Co. of London, built the St. Kitts Sugar Factory, to handle all the island's cane. Sail soon gave way to steam - and carried vast quantities of St. Kitts sugar to all parts of Europe. Profits remained high, as the product was (and still is) rated 'the world's finest & purest Natural Cane Sugar'.

Banky-Banky and the Monkey Jar

In1986 - canefields and factory were merged into one processing unit. Cane is now grown on 44 estates and many canefields still carry the names given to them by the early settlers. One can only guess at the stories, the tragedies and the strange circumstances that created such field names as 'JUMBIE HOLE 9'; 'CANADA MAN 'O WAR'; 'UPPER DUNG PIT'; 'BIG RUNAWAY GRAVE'; 'COOPER & SHOP CORN'; 'TEN-PENNY GARDEN'; 'RABBIT WALL'; 'TWELVE & SALT WATER'; 'CON-OLLY'; 'HILDENS WELL AND NANNY WORK'; 'SOLDIER HILL & LONG RUN'; 'UPPER JACK SPANIARD'; 'BANKY-BANKY'; 'PINNEL AND MADAME PUCE'; 'MONKEY JAR'; 'CARPOON LONG RUN'; 'WEAKNESS' - and 'LITTLE NANNY COFFIN'.

Nature's own sculptural landscape masterpieces, often dwarf even the massive cane-hauling tractors of the sugar harvesters as they work on this vital crop.

Photo - Frank Sharman

Illustration - Stuart Orchard/Dawn Carey

Photo - Livingston Jackson

Skilled Cane Cutters, gathering in the waving green sugarcane stalks by hand, often prove to be more efficient and productive than any machine devised by Man.

Lost Records - Missing Tips

Under the original owners, some unusually high sugar yields often resulted. Due to the lack of proper written records, many of the old 'tips and techniques' have become lost forever. Almost everything was done by word of mouth and possibly recorded in note books which have long since been destroyed or lost.

Sugar City's Local Pride

The current St. Kitts Sugar Manufacturing Corporation aims at standardisation, to maintain the island's fame as 'the home of the world's finest natural cane sugar'. The popular Caribbean nickname for St. Kitts is - 'Sugar City' - and all Kittitians are justly proud of it

Game, 'Sett' and Match

Cane is grown by planting 'setts' (pieces of 4-5 month old cane about 15" long), in furrows. The furrow is re-covered and the soil compacted. Planting in St. Kitts takes place during the Spring & Autumn (Fall) months and cane is ready for harvesting in about fourteen months. After the harvest, fertiliser is applied to the cane 'stools', which obligingly, simply regrow again.

Crop, Crop and Re-Crop
This 're-grown' cane is ready for a second harvesting in another10-12 months. This process is repeated until the sugar yields drop. Usually four to five crops can be taken, before the cane is planted afresh.

The Sugar-Land Express makes a Round Trip
The sugar railway was established in 1912 - a mere one mile section of straight track from the Factory to the Sugar Pier on the Caribbean side of the island. A four mile line to Palmetto Point and a 7 mile track to Christ Church were then laid down - giving a 'Y' shape system. In 1925, this was extended to complete a 30 mile, circular single line track around the main island.

Go Directly to Bed
Level crossings and steel girder bridges, with 50' and 60' spans at Stonefort River, the Hermitage, Old Road, Godwin, Crabtree, Fig Tree, Belmont, Lynches, Christ Church, Soldier Ghaut, Grange and Cayon, were built. Then the 30 inch gauge, rail sections were secured to 2" steel troughed sleepers spaced at about two feet centres, without ballast, laid directly on the road-bed.

The powerful sugarcane tractors are a familiar sight around the island of St. Kitts, during the harvesting season, as they haul in the giant wagons of fresh-cut cane.

Photo - Livingston Jackson

Photo - Livingston Jackson

The charming little Sugar Cane Railroad wends its way around the entire island, through fields of freshly grown cane, gathering in the many tons of cut sugar crop.

The Train Now Landing on the Main Runway...

The average gradient of the tiny 30" gauge track is approx. 1% - with curves ranging between 2 and 8 degrees of curve on the permanentway. A limited number of short turnouts accomodate defective wagons. Two diversions were created later, to allow for the original and the present 7600' Golden Rock Airport runway and extensions.

'Come in, Number Twelve - it's Cane-time'

All sugar train movements are handled by Traffic Control, with VHF radio links between the Train Drivers, the Marshalling Yards, the tiny 'Stations' and the Signalmen scattered around the island. Despite its modest size,this highly efficient network can handle the island-wide movements of up to 3,000 tons of sugar cane every day.

A few technical details may be of interest to both tourist and also visiting Railway Buffs - who are all welcome to go and tour the Sugar Factory. **For next tour times - Call #465-8157.** Thousands of visitors every year, enjoy the highly informative guided trip.

Stately palms and growing sugar cane, blend into a delightful island pastoral scene.

LOCOMOTIVE TYPES AND HORSEPOWER

NO:	MAKE/TYPE		YEAR	H.P.	MAIN JOB
1.	Hunslet	0-3-0	1958	101	Mainline Haulage
2.	Hunslet	0-3-0	1958	101	Mainline Haulage
3.	Hunslet	0-3-0	1958	101	Mainline Haulage
4.	Hunslet	0-3-0	1958	101	Mainline Haulage
5.	Hunslet	0-3-0	1958	101	Mainline Haulage
6.	Hunslet	0-3-0	1958	101	Mainline Haulage
7.	Hunslet	0-3-0	1958	101	Mainline Haulage
9.	Ruston	0-3-0	——	40	Yard Shunting
10.	Ruston	0-3-0	——	100	Mainline Haulage
11.	Ruston	0-3-0	——	100	Mainline Haulage
12.	Armstrong	0-2-0	1934	125	Haulage to Pier
13.	Davenport	0-3-0	——	145	Short Haul
14.	Ruston	0-2-0	——	40	Yard Shunting
15.	Hunslet	0-3-0	——	150	Mainline Haulage
16.	Whitcomb	0-3-0	——	145	Tipper/Storage
17.	Whitcomb	0-3-0	——	145	Mainline Haulage
18.	Ruston	0-3-0	——	100	Mainline Haulage
19.	Ruston	0-3-0	——	100	Mainline Haulage
20.	Ruston	0-3-0	——	100	Mainline Haulage

NB. The Sugar Railmen's 'mascot' is old Number 12, the original 1934 Armstrong and still in daily use, carrying thousands of tons of bulk sugar from the factory to the Sugar Pier for shipment. Current Rolling Stock includes: 725 (3 Ton) Cane Wagons, 49 Mud Wagons, 25 Bagasse Wagons, 18 Sugar Bins (9 groups), 5 Flat Bed Bogies and 4 Molasses Tankers. Not all Engines' histories are fully recorded.

The Sugar Railmen's mascot is old Number 12, the original 1934, 125 horse-power Armstrong Locomotive, used daily to haul the finished product to the Sugar Pier.

Photo - Frank Sharman

Rawlins Plantation Mill, one of several beautifully restored original stone mills, displays the owner's high regard for the island's unique history and tradition.

A Mere 8.7 Million 1 pound Bags - for starters!
Ordered in 1911, the Sugar Factory was quickly assembled, tested and finally commissioned in the following year. It had a grinding capacity of a mere 28 tons of sugarcane per hour, but still produced 3,891 tons (8,715,840 pounds) of finished sugar - supplied then, by about one third of the island's Sugar Estates.

The Hand-Built Railroad
Soon, the Factory had built a Landing Pier, laid over nine miles of the Railway System and put down nearly five miles of Water Piping, way up to the source in the mountains. And all done then, by hard manual labour!

Up to 112 Million Bags? - and still more to come!
Forty-three years later, in 1955, production was up by nearly 400% - to 110 tons per hour and the factory produced almost 50,000 tons of finished sugar, from just over 400,000 tons of sugar cane. Imagine how many stalks of sugarcane that represents! How many of the world's favourite cups of tea or coffee, would it sweeten? And how many jars of 'Mum's Strawberry Jam'! **So why not buy a Souvenir Pack - to take home!**

Not as simple as Mum's Strawberry Jam!
Although the process of making sugar is apparently a relatively simple matter. i.e. Growing and Cutting the Cane; Collecting and Crushing the stalks; Boiling up the Raw Sucrose extracted; Refining the now syrupy 'Process Juice'; and then Crystallising to obtain the finished product. It's not quite as simple as watching Mother make some Strawberry Jam for the family!

The Patience of Job - the Wisdom of Solomon
The complex art of balancing out the daily problems of the many varying production rates - Canefields, Rail deliveries, Crushing Mills, Juice Boilers, Strainers, Clarifiers & Centrifuges - requires the skill, expertise and attention to detail, that only a highly experienced and first-class Sugar Industry Manager can command.

Day and Night - under the Caribbean Sun
During Cane Cutting season, when the freshly cut crop is arriving hourly, by the train-load - the men at the St. Kitts Sugar Factory work virtually round-the-clock, and the mournful cry of the 'shift-change whistle', often echos eerily through the early-breaking dawn.

The charming, cloud-capped sister island of Nevis, forms a beautiful backdrop to another stunning example of the natural beauty of the St. Kitts landscape.

Photo - Livingston Jackson

CHAPTER EIGHT

Brimstone Hill - the mightiest fortress

'Do you know that Brimstone Hill is the main thing for which St. Kitts is world famous?', asked a visiting Norwegian yachtsman, who frequently calls here.

A Mighty Block of Basalt

The question started thoughts as to what it is about this unique historical monument, that has led to Brimstone Hill Fortress being so widely acclaimed, both as a National Park and a unique Museum. The geological origins of this massive basalt-based hilltop, often called the 'Gibraltar of the New World', are in no way related to the surrounding mountain ranges. It emerged, in solitary splendour, from far below ground, during a later period of intense volcanic activity, far back in the pre-history of St. Kitts.

Sugar Cane and Six Islands

This 38-acre Fortress is situated on the upper slopes of an 800 foot high mountain with superb views all around. Six other islands can be seen on a clear day and the scenery ranges from Rain Forests, which cap the mountains, through the gently sloping lands going down to the sea covered with the traditional patterns of greens and browns that reveal sugar cane cultivation. Picturesque towns and villages are included in the scenery and these landscapes are all framed by the blue Caribbean Sea. Brimstone Hill's scenery is a photographer's paradise.

Cannonballs from the Skies

Brimstone Hill was first fortified in the year 1690. The British 'Redcoats' mounted mighty cannons there, specifically to bombard the French who were in possession of a British coastal fort below them.

Epic Battles on Land and Sea

The work was done in a desultory fashion and when the French invaded in approximately 1782, the Fortress was far from complete. In spite of this, approximately 950 defenders, which included soldiers of two British regiments and 350 local Militia, who were hopelessly outnumbered and outgunned from the start, resisted for approximately one month before they finally surrendered.

The Redcoats Move Out

The French then held the Fortress until the Treaty of Versailles was signed in 1783, when St. Kitts was among the West Indian islands returned to Britain. The years 1783 to 1794 saw an intense period of reconstruction and development and most of the upper work, including the imposing Prince of Wales Bastion and the massive Citadel (Fort George), were then completed. However, in 1853 the Fortress was abandoned by the British and there was a fifty year period of neglect and vandalism. Finally, from early in this century, more interest was taken in the site, particularly by a Historic Sites Committee.

The mighty ramparts of Brimstone Hill, where massive cannons stand guard, overlook the straits that lead to the Dutch island of St. Eustatius.

Photo - Livingston Jackson

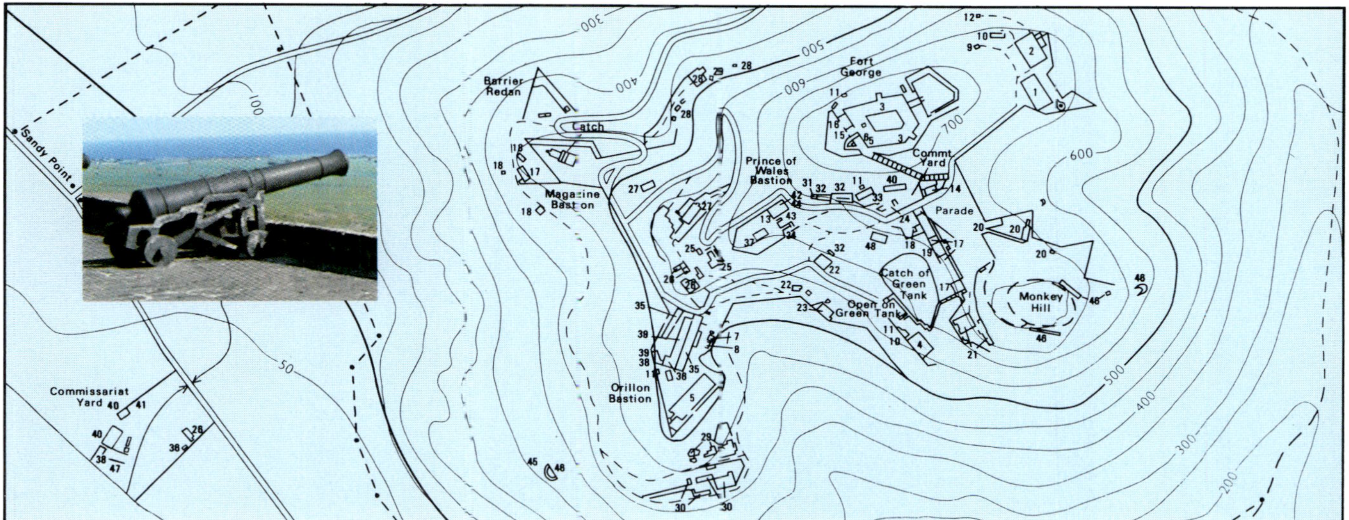

Brimstone Hill Fortress, St. Kitts

West Indies

REFERENCES

1 No 4 Barrack
2 No 5 Barrack
3 Fort George Barrack
4 Artillery Barrack
5 Hospital
6 Deadhouse
7 PMG's Office
8 Hospital Steward's Quarters
9 Washing Sheds
10 Cook Houses
11 Privies Men's
12 Women's Privy
13 Guard Houses
14 Sentry Sheds
15 Lunatics
16 Mental House
17 Regimental Officers' Quarters
18 Officers' Quarters
19 Officers Garrison Mess Room
20 Commandant's Quarters & Officers Mess Room
21 Artillery Officers Quarters & Mess Room
22 Staff Sergeants Quarters & Mess Room
23 Ordnance Clerks Quarters & Mess Room
24 Commissariat Issuers Quarters & Mess Room
25 Fort Adjutant Quarters & Officers Mess Room
26 Assistant Surgeons (or 2nd Medical Officers) Quarters & Mess Room
27 Reserve Engineers Quarters & Mess Room
28 Principal Medical Officer's Quarters & Mess Room
29 Clerk of Works Quarters & Mess Room
30 Deputy Storekeepers Quarters & Mess Room
31 Barrack Sergeants Quarters & Mess Room
32 Building used as Canteen
33 Garrison Stable
34 Powder Magazine
35 Ordnance Storehouses
36 Ordnance Coopers Quarters
37 Artillery Storehouse
38 Engineer Storehouse
39 Engineer Workshops
40 Commissariat Storehouses
41 Commissariat Bakery
42 Brigade Office
43 Ordnance Office
44 RL Engineer Office
45 Old Lime Store
46 Disused Outworks
47 Ruined Sea Wall
48 Condemned Magazine

Where Queen and Cannon met

In 1965, a Society for the Restoration of Brimstone Hill was formed, which has spearheaded a great deal of restoration work. This has now been reconstituted as the Brimstone Hill Fortress National Park Society. The National Park was inaugurated by Her Majesty Queen Elizabeth the Second, during her1985 official visit with His Royal Highness the Duke of Edinburgh.

A Network of Military Genius

There is a great deal to see, admire and wonder about at Brimstone Hill,-including the expertise of the planners in creating sites for the various bastions, in designing buildings that fit so perfectly into the surrounding scenery, and also in designing a roadway and various paths which interconnect all sections of the complex. The water collection systems at Brimstone Hill are a study in themselves. It should always be borne in mind that Brimstone Hill was a complete military community. Consider, the awesome amount of labour involved in the construction of the stone buildings. Most of the work was done by slave labour, but the stones show the care of the builders.

Legend has it that the giant cannons of the Brimstone Hill Fortress (now a National Park), could easily hurl cannonballs into marauding ships attacking Basseterre.

Photo - Frank Sharman

Photo - Livingston Jackson

The beautifully restored Citadel, housing many special exhibits, dominates the crown of Brimstone Hill - built on a natural prehistoric volcanic upthrust of basalt.

Swords can be beaten...

The ancient and mighty cannons of Brimstone Hill will never again be fired in anger. The Fortress today is probably the most peaceful place on the tranquil island of St. Kitts. A mighty monument and a subtle reminder to visitors that 'Swords can still be beaten into plowshares'. Historic sites have a key role to play in the economic development of even the smallest countries. The use of such sites can create places of education and enjoyment for both visitors and citizens. When research and historical interpretation are added, a vital sense of national pride and heritage can be created, particularly in the school children and young people of this relatively new nation. For the visitor, Brimstone Hill is a monument to a past age.

A Breath of History

A visit to Brimstone Hill is an unforgettable experience. A breath of heroic history that brings the past alive. One can stand quietly in the stillness of the Citadel and almost hear again the clatter of weapons, the boom of the mighty cannons and the officer's shouted commands from a military age long past.

Cannon Balls, Buttons and Maps
A museum was opened at Fort George on January 26, 1982 and good progress has been made ever since. With the restoration of several rooms, the museum now offers special sections which feature the past involvements of several nations in Brimstone Hill's glorious but chequered past.

International Co-operation - at last!
Despite historic national differences, the British, French and American rooms, were assembled by willing local and overseas public cooperation from many nationalities. Generous donations of letters, uniforms and many other historical objects of special interest, have made this project a reality.

Help Us to Save Our Heritage
When you visit Brimstone Hill Fortress, we urge you to be generous in helping us to preserve and improve its defences against the ravages of modern day life. Your contribution will be used wisely - and you will have the satisfying assurance that you have helped us to firmly preserve our tiny nation's fragile national heritage.

The fascinating stamps of St. Kitts, capture the colourful uniforms of the many brave regiments who gave their services in the defence of Brimstone Hill.

Courtesy St. Kitts Philatelic Bureau

CHAPTER NINE

Flora and Fauna - a tropical paradise

The flora and fauna of St. Kitts truly resembles a tropical paradise. This small island has an incredible variety of plants and wildlife and some researchers have described the habitat as resembling a 'miniature Africa'. The habitat itself ranges from sparse, savanna-like grasslands to the lush mountain Rain Forest, which surrounds the central area of the island and an inactive volcano with a crater that is often water-filled.

A Thorny Problem

The Southeast Peninsula provides a different and unique environment with its sparsely separated small trees and shrubs. Acacia, with its sharp thorns, is found everywhere throughout the grassy areas. Also found on the Southeast Penisula is the Great Salt Pond, which adds another unique twist to this habitat. Such a diversity in the environment has helped to bring about the different animal life found here, many of them having been brought centuries ago.

A Long Tail of Gold

Wild mammals include the African Green Monkey (Vervet), the White-Tailed Deer, and a very large population of Mongooses. The African Green Vervet Monkey has adapted extremely well to both the Rain Forest and the savanna, with its numbers rising well into the thousands. These monkeys move in troops varying in size from a half dozen to two or three dozens. They are small primates ranging from a 6" high, 5 lb. juvenile, to an adult male of around 25 lbs., growing up to 36" in height. Their tail is longer than their body and their color is more golden than green as their name implies. Not easily tamed, monkeys bare their teeth if threatened and have a fierce bite.

The Island Baby Deer

The White-Tailed Deer (Odecoleus sp.) were brought here at the turn of this century for hunting purposes, but were eventually released and allowed to live in peace. These deer are not as abundant as the monkeys and are mostly to be found on the Southeast Peninsula. The young fawns are born with a black mask and white spots going up and down their back, both distinctive markings fade as they mature. The young are about 3-5 lbs. at birth and most adults do not weigh more than 60 lbs. This species is not as large as those in North America, although related.

No Snakes Here on our Paradise Island

Captured in a pensive mood, this young 2 month-old Green Vervet Monkey, is typical of the many shy primates of this species that inhabit our island paradise.

Photo - Frank Sharman

The Mongoose (Norway rat), and many other small mammals and rodents are found throughout the island. They often pose more than a minor nuisance to gardens and land-resting birds. The shy and swift little Mongoose, with its elongated body, was originally first introduced to rid the island of all snakes. Today, these now-unemployed creatures can best be seen darting across the roads, between the many canefields.

Photo - Livingston Jackson

This rarely seen example of a baby White-Tailed Deer, lives in the virtually uninhabited South East Peninsula region of this beautiful island.

How to tell Sheep from Goats

Domestic animals are characteristic of a highly agricultural based economy. There are many varieties of cattle, used for meat and milk production, as well as sheep, goats, pigs, chickens and small wild turkeys. The sheep on the island do not have a woolly coat, making them very hard to distinguish from the goats. One rule of thumb that may help in differentiating them is that goats have their tail up (like a letter 't'), whilst sheep have their tail down (like a letter 'p').

Birds of a Feather

St. Kitts is an ornithologist's delight. Some of the best mixes of avian species can be found here, ranging from the water birds that feed on the marine life they find on the coral reefs and unattended fishing nets, to the small land based Caribbean bullfinches.

A Cow's Best Friend

The most prevalent bird on the island is the Cattle egret (Bubulcus ibis). These stream-lined white birds can be seen soaring around the cattle, and often resting on their backs, where they feed on parasites.

Stamps - Courtesy St. Kitts Philatelic Bureau

Delightfully depicted on these 'miniature works of art', are a pleasing selection of the multitude of brightly coloured birds, many of whom live deep in the Rain Forests.

Rapid Wings Humming Along

Of the smaller species, there are countless colourful Common Ground Doves (Columbina passerina) and Tropical Mocking Birds (Mimis gilvus). Hummingbirds (Trochilidae) are abundant, having colours from metallic green to a dark purple. These small birds are about 3 inches long and feed only on nectar and small insects. Their habitat ranges from town flower beds to the Rain Forest and Crater. Another common island bird is the Bananaquit or Banana Bird (Banaquit coereba Flaveola). Bright yellow with black markings and a long, thin beak, they feed mainly on fruit but have been known to consume rice, bread, sugar and vegetables when dining at the tables of some bird loving residents. Other land birds commonly seen include the Red Tailed Hawk (Buteo jamaicensis) and the American Kestrel (Falco sparverius).

Diving for Dinner

The water birds include The Laughing Gull (Larus atricilla) and the Brown Pelican (Pelecanus occidentalis). The predatory Pelicans often dive from heights of close to 75 feet for their meals.

Greedy Gulls Stealing a Mouthful
The lazy gull sometimes lands on the back of the Pelican in an effort to snatch a small piece of fish that might be left behind. Another bird that lives from the water, is the black and white coloured Magnificent Frigatebird (Frigata magnificens) which can often be seen on the wing over beaches and ponds. On your excursion to Banana Bay, try to get close to uninhabited Booby Island where you will find its largest inhabitant, Sula leucogaster - commonly known as the Brown Booby Bird.

Sugar Snitchers at Breakfast
As you sip your breakfast tea or coffee, you may catch sight of the Lesser Antillean Bullfinch, or Sugar bird (Loxigilla noctis) sneaking a quick beakful of sugar.

Botanist's Delight
St. Kitts also boasts a host of flower and tree species that are pleasing to the eye. The Amaryllis, or Barbados Lily (Hippeastrum puniceum) is sure to be seen during the winter, for this red trumpet shaped flower is a hardy species.

The most commonly seen animals on the island, are undoubtably the many types of domestic and semi-wild Goats - most of which appear to roam freely on the streets.

Photo - Livingston Jackson

Photo - Frank Sharman

The dramatic beauty of the Heliconia is but one of many examples of eye-catching tropical flowers, trees and shrubs to be found everywhere on this island paradise.

Over 200 Species of Hibiscus

Both the Hibiscus (Hibiscus spp.) and Coral Hibiscus (H. schizopetalus) plants grow in abundance. There are at least 200 species that can be found here and also throughout the Leeward Islands. The Spider Lily (hymenocallis caribaea) can be identified by its unusual flower pattern. The six petals are white, and very thin, while the green stamens are longer and more distinctly pendulous in shape.

Christmas Decorations for the Taking

On St. Kitts, one does not have to go to the florists, in order to buy a Poinsetta (Euphorbia pulcherema) for decorating the house during the Christmas holiday season. The species thrives extremely well, here sometimes growing to heights of up to 12 feet. Other common flowers, used for house decoration, include rare and beautiful Orchids (Orchidaceae), the colourful Oleander (Nerium oleander), Mexican Creeper or Coralito (Antigonon leptopus), Heliconia (Helconia spp), Anthurium Lilies of several colours (Anthurium andraeanum) and masses of beautiful Bouganvillea (Bougainvillea spp).

Flaming Red Poinciana

One must journey outside of Basseterre to gain a full appreciation for the many beautiful trees. One of the most breathtaking is the Poinciana or Flamboyant tree (Delonix regia). When in flower it is characterised by bursts of red blossoms in wide-spreading crowns. This tree's flowers are about 4 inches in diameter and the fruits are produced in flat pods about 24 inches long. The Poinciana is said to be named after the French nobleman Count de Poincy, who as an amateur botanist, imported many exotic plants into the island of St. Kitts during the several periods of French rule.

Butterflies and Pagodas

A smaller species is the Bauhinia, or Butterfly tree (Bauhinia purpurea), which is distinguished by its cow hoof-shaped leaves. The Frangipani, or Pagoda tree (Plumeria sp.) is characterised by its spreading branches and reddish-orange to pink blossoms. It is particularly attractive due to the pleasant scent produced by its flowers. The large Jacaranda Fern tree (Jacaranda acutifolia) has a bell-shaped purplish hued flower and the blooms rise in clusters.

Not often seen, this rare example of a young island Hawk prepares for its first flight, after being treated for a damaged wing, by a caring veterinary student.

Photo - Keith Gold

Bleep-Bloop, Bleep-Bloop - all night long.
To northerners, accustomed only to the muted roar of late night city traffic or to the deathly silence of small town suburban nights - the most noticable night sound in St. Kitts is the constant 'bleep-bloop' cry of the tiny, thumb-nail sized Tree Frogs, often mingled with the see-saw rasping sounds of the cricket's wings.

When is a Toad not a Toad?
Regardless of species, almost all St. Kitts islanders refer to both Frogs, and their half-cousins, the Toads - as 'frogs'. Despite the fact that real toads are many times the size of the authentic and minute, bright green, tree-living frogs - this misnomer is now firmly set in the local Kittitian vocabulary.

Now we can reveal the answer - on camera!
With great patience, we persuaded an authentic local Toad to pose for our cameras - and although we were unable to charm any Tree Frogs to join him, we can assure you that one would need over two dozen of them, all playing 'piggy-back' - to rival him in size.

Although the islanders refer to both frogs and toads as 'Frogs', this superb specimen of a Toad (Xenopus sp.), does not appear to mind this minor error.

Photo - Livingston Jackson

CHAPTER TEN

Food, Drink and Shelter - a tradition of hospitality

If paradise is not here.....we must be very close to it! St. Kitts possesses many hotels - and each one is ready to make sure your stay on 'our island home', is totally beautiful. Kittitians are fairly shy people by nature, but they still have a way of making you feel at home.

Watersports, West Indian Wimbledon & Lady Luck

There are all types of accommodation on the island, ranging from the comfortable, air-conditioned 5-room **'On The Square' Guesthouse** (Tel: 465-2485), located in the town centre on Independence Square itself - to several more sophisticated and larger modern hotels - like the breath-takingly beautiful **Ocean Terrace Inn** or the 'all-inclusive' **Jack Tar Village** which features many Tours, a Casino, Golf, Tennis and Watersports.

Do try 'De Local Goat Water, Man!'

If your idea of a visit to the Caribbean conjures up a dream of coconuts, mangoes, papayas, guavas, soursop and guineps, then your dreams can come true. We have all that - and a lot more. St. Kitts now offers a growing choice of restaurants catering to both tourists and locals. Most can offer the visitor both International and local West Indian cuisine - with some St. Kitts specialities that you will find hard to resist. Do try the popular 'Goatwater' (meat) soup, West Indian Stew, 'Souse', Pumpkin Fritters, Breadfruit Slices, Roti, 'Conkie' and many others.

Why there are no 'Tourists' in St. Kitts

It is often said that St. Kitts has everything the other Caribbean islands can offer - except the crowds! Maybe it is because we regard all our visitors as our 'guests' and not as 'mere tourists', here to spend a dollar.

A Distinctly French Flavour
The oldest hotel on the island, is undoubtably the beautiful **Fairview Inn** (Tel: 465-2472). It was once an 18th century Great House, built to house the Commanding Officer of the French army in St. Kitts.

Just a bit of Fixin' Up
Proprietors Freddy and Betty Lam purchased the property in the early 1960's and set about making it into a first class resort. The Great House was renovated and a gallery added. Guest cottages were built around the beautiful grounds, all of which teem with flowers - all lovingly planted by Betty Lam.

Let's Dance 'til Dawn
Elegant green lawns surround the 32-room hotel, which features poolside Dining and Dancing. Fairview Inn is a favourite island spot and the regular venue, at noon every Thursday, for local Rotary Club meetings.

Take a Hike after Breakfast
Fairview offers superb views over the Caribbean, whilst its nearby Ottley's Hill, has some of the best hiking.

The magnificent verandas of the Fairview Inn are well sited to capture the cooling breezes - and enjoy the most splendid views of the calm Caribbean Sea.

Photo - Livingston Jackson

Photo - Frank Sharman

The tumbling tropical terraces of the Ocean Terrace Inn overlook the most splendid views of the Great Bay of Basseterre - clear across to the sister island of Nevis.

The **Ocean Terrace Inn** (Tel: 465-2754/2380) nestles into neatly landscaped, terraced gardens, overlooking the Bay of Basseterre, the blue Caribbean & the island of Nevis. It features its own harbour and a fleet of boats making daily runs to its sister hotel, the Banana Bay Beach Resort. Trips & watersports are free to guests.

Unashamed Personal Luxury

With 52 delightful rooms, all with 12-channel cable TV and air-conditioning, the OTI has truly found the perfect balance between a quiet efficiency and unashamed luxury, with the personal touch provided by its charming owners Colin and Leslie Pereira.

Pepperpot & Goat Water

During the day, one can relax in the gardens and enjoy the two fresh-water swimming pools or the jacuzzi. In the evening, after the sun sets, relax by the Calypso Bar, where you can watch the varied live nightly entertainment of Steel Bands, Fashion Shows and Afro West Indian dancing - or dine at the hotel's very popular International Cuisine restaurant, which will also delight you with its many Caribbean specialities.

The beautifully secluded **Banana Bay Beach Resort** (Tel: 469-5729), is the sister hotel of the Ocean Terrace Inn. Located at the tip of the Southeast Peninsula, it is one of those truly unspoilt corners of paradise for which we all yearn but so rarely find. So, if you are seeking peace, quiet and a relaxing atmosphere, a visit to Banana Bay is a must. Its two beautiful sandy beaches are surrounded by acres of magnificently unspoilt countryside. A walker's paradise!

Calling Zebra One.....
Accessible only by boat, you will be transported from the OTI's private Wharf, down the coast to Whitehouse Bay and then continue your journey from there onwards by the 'Zebra Safari' Land Rover, past the Great Salt Pond to the quiet peace of Banana Bay, where you can enjoy windsurfing, sailing, snorkeling or relaxing on the secluded and palm-fringed beach.

Exclusive Luxury from charming hosts
The friendly management will ensure that your stay at the BBBR will be a memorable one. Exclusive luxury is the keynote at Banana Bay, making dreams come true!

Luxury and seclusion, combined with total relaxation on the beautiful sandy beaches of the Banana Bay Beach Resort, make this a perfect and private spot.

Photo - Livingston Jackson

Photo - Livingston Jackson

Clustered around a calm lagoon and framed by a magnificent Golf Course, one finds the Royal St. Kitts - Jack Tar Village - the island's successful 'all-inclusive' resort.

Well tended grounds, activity areas and comfortable villa style accommodations, give **Jack Tar Village - Royal St. Kitts** (Tel: 465-8651) a very sophisticated atmosphere. All 250 spacious and tastefully furnished rooms are air-conditioned, with patios or verandas and double or king sized beds. Jack Tar Village is the island's only 'all inclusive' resort and all meals, snacks, drinks, wines, activities, sports, equipment (plus use and instructions), nightly live entertainment and dancing - are totally free to all registered guests.

Casino, Beauty Salon, Disco - and much more
The hub of the resort is a large two storey main building that features an open air Garden Restaurant & Bar, a fully air-conditioned Dining Room, Casino, Disco, Lounge, Beauty Salon and Gift Shop. There are four tennis courts (even for night play), a Golf Course - plus two swimming pools and a Pool Bar and Grill.

Hit the Beaches for Fun in the Sun
On the nearby Atlantic beach, is the Cabana Beach Bar, whilst on the Caribbean beach, just a short ride away on the free JTV shuttle, is the busy Watersports Office.

The Golden Lemon (Tel: 465-7260) is located in Dieppe Bay and created by Arthur Leaman, one-time Decorating Editor of 'House & Garden' magazine. On finding a ramshackle 17th century house, set back amidst a coconut grove on a black beach, he converted it into a beautiful and luxurious 'secret' retreat.

Private Pools and Whirling Fans

The two-storey house, with its covered galleries, has spacious high-ceilinged rooms filled with antiques. No two rooms are alike but all feature canopied four-poster beds, slow-whirling ceiling fans, one-of-a-kind pieces and an abundance of fresh flowers. The walled garden holds a fresh water swimming pool - and six of the Lemon's luxury suites also offer private pools.

18th Century Elegance comes alive

The food is excellent, combining Creole, International and American influences. Travel back in time....enjoy a candle lit meal in18th century surroundings. Care is taken on all individual diets and you are waited on by a well-trained staff. 'Sophisticated and Elegant' are words often used describing the Lemon and its guests.

Eighteenth Century living is the keynote at the elegant and world- famous Golden Lemon, which features magnificent four poster beds, antiques and original prints.

Photo - Livingston Jackson

Photo - Livingston Jackson

Acre after acre of unspoilt pasture surround Rawlins Plantation, the beautifully restored family home of Phillip Walwyn, who owns this delightful hillside inn.

The small luxurious nine room, **Rawlins Plantation** (Tel. 465-6221/2098) is owned personally & managed by Philip and Frances Walwyn. It is a very special place, being extremely peaceful and particularly beautiful. The Inn itself, is set amid 25 acres of magnificently colourful gardens and unspoilt pasture lands - at 350 feet above sea level. It also enjoys panoramic views over thousands of unspoilt acres.

Rawlins' Splendid Sugar Mill

Behind Rawlins Plantation, the mountains rise to nearly 4,000 feet and the Crater is close by. The Rawlins' gardens are rated as some of the finest in the entire Caribbean, with a splendidly converted Sugar Mill, flanked by masses of colourful flowering shrubs.

Pure Air, Fine Food and Just Lazing

Rawlins Plantation caters to a wide range of ages, the common denominator being the desire for peace, pure air, fine food and beautiful surroundings. Tennis, croquet and horse-back riding are available at Rawlins - and the area is absolutely perfect for Hiking or for just simply lazing around and totally relaxing.

Photo - Livingston Jackson

When the sun sets over the Caribbean Sea - the hot night music begins its captivating beat - as the various hotels begin their nightly entertainment.

Relaxing over a cool local Carib beer or a spicy Rum Punch, visitors can soak up the vibrant atmosphere of the island's night life - before sampling our cuisine.

Entertainment ranges from native drummers and folk dancing groups - to steel bands, batik and other fashion shows - plus the more modern disco-beat.

Photo - Frank Sharman

Photo - Frank Sharman

Situated beside the sparkling clear waters of the Caribbean Beach, the Frigate Bay Beach Hotel's inviting fresh water pool forms a centerpiece to their luxurious units.

In one of the most beautiful areas of St. Kitts, they have created a resort that offers comfort and charm.

On the Edge of the Green, beside the Beach

The **Frigate Bay Beach Hotel** (Tel: 465-8935/8936), nestles amid rolling hills of multi-coloured rock and overlooks the nearby golden sandy beach at Frigate Bay. Adjoining the 18 hole Championship Golf Course, this elegant hotel offers a choice of large airy rooms and self-contained suites - all with private balconies.

Take a Sip as you Dip

All the rooms overlook the large freshwater Swimming Pool, where you can float lazily on your back, whilst deciding what to choose when you paddle up to the Dip 'N Sip Pool Bar, to sit on one of those handy underwater stools.

Split-level Luxury as you Dine

The interesting split-level Restaurant offers a very extensive menu of delicacies and features a variety of International Entrees, delicious Buffets and West Indian dishes - with romantic candle-lit dining.

A small and private beach village, nestled on the edge of the sand dunes, which fringe the Atlantic Ocean, sounds to many like pure paradise.

A Home from Home - with all Comforts

The popular self-catering **Sun 'N Sand Beach Village** (Tel: 465-8037/8038) features a cluster of small villas, all self-contained and spaciously grouped around a relaxing freshwater Pool. Particularly suitable for families, especially those with children, visitors planning a long stay - and small groups of friends. The Sun 'N Sand villas & studio apartments are all very nicely laid out, with comfortable air-conditioned bedrooms. A neat compact kitchenette, a useful lounge with ceiling fan and private little verandas make these beachside villas a true 'home from home'.

Everything You Need - Close at Hand

On the site, which is adjacent to a splendid18 Hole Championship Golf Course, close to a Pizza Parlour and a short walk from the Royal St. Kitts Casino, you'll find a well stocked Mini-Mart, a Beach Bar Restaurant and a handful of very useful shops for most daily needs.

A few short steps through the sand dunes at the Sun 'N Sand Beach Village, brings you to the long and virtually deserted magnificence of North Frigate Bay beach.

Photo - S & S

Photo - Livingston Jackson

The picturesque and busy marina at Pelican Cove, is home to the Fisherman's Wharf, one of the island's most popular fresh Seafood Restaurants.

On the beach, just across the road from the Ocean Terrace Inn's landscaped gardens, you will find the OTI's popular **Fisherman's Wharf Bar & Seafood Restaurant** - on a waterfront jetty, right on the sea!.

The Fleet's In - at Pelican Cove Marina
This also the base for the Ocean Terrace Inn's fleet of fast boats, which can cater for all your water sports & marine requirements - from Deep Sea Fishing, Bottom Fishing, SCUBA diving and Snorkeling trips to Moonlight cruises, secluded Beach Picnics or trips to the Banana Bay Beach Resort - (free to OTI guests).

Chowder anyone?
Fisherman's Wharf (Tel: 465-4121/4122) is best known to tourists and locals for its fine and fresh local seafood restaurant and bar where you can enjoy "the catch of the day", a grilled lobster and why not try their delicious 'Conch Chowder'? All this and lots more, right there by a charming waterfront. The Fisherman's Wharf is also the home of the **Conch Shell Boutique** where you will find a range of exotic island clothing, handcrafted gifts and accessories.

Splendid Views from the Top of the Rock
Dominating the rocky bluff, to the west of the town and completing the sweep of the Bay of Basseterre - the **Fort Thomas Hotel** (Tel: 465-2695) presents 64 comfortable and spacious air-conditioned rooms.

Private Balconies and a Free Beach Bus
Each features two double beds and a private balcony, from which one captures splendid sunsets and sweeping panoramas of our lush mountains or sparkling blue seas. Beside the large swimming pool, the casual Terrace Bar offers a range of exotic Caribbean thirst-quenchers to those guests too busy relaxing to board the free beach shuttle bus.

Carve Yourself a Caribbean Conference
Carefully run by Hotel Management International, the hotel lives up to its motto - 'We enjoy saying Welcome' and welcomes many Conferences to its thoughtful facilities. Delegates, visiting businessmen and vacation guests also appreciate the wide and tasty range of the international and local Creole cuisine of its restaurant, which features a splendid Carvery and Salad Bar.

Perfectly situated on the Fortlands rock bluff, the Fort Thomas Hotel captures the warm Caribbean sunshine every day. No wonder its giant pool is so popular.

Photo - Livingston Jackson

Illustration - Spencer Cameron Gallery

The Spencer Cameron Gallery and the Ballahoo Restaurant share the same quaint 'olde- worlde' premises overlooking Basseterre's busy town centre and The Circus.

Limin' Time at the Ballahoo

Just sit and watch the world go by. **The Ballahoo Restaurant** (Tel: 465-4197) is the place to do just that. On the Gallery overlooking the Circus, relax in cool comfort while you enjoy good food and generous drinks. Ballahoo specials include Parrotfish, locally grown Shrimp, Steak and Lobster. Sandwiches and snacks are also available to accompany a drink. Do be sure to try one of their thirst-quenching local fruit juices. Friday nights at the Ballahoo are often Mexican nights and offers you a chance to sample their international cooking. Apart from its popular Long Balcony, they also have plenty of indoor dining space.

Right Next Door - Art Galore!

Adjoining the Ballahoo is the **Spencer Cameron Art Gallery** (Tel: 465-4047). Spencer Cameron offers a wide range of local artwork from original Paintings to superb Limited Edition Lithographs. Typical West Indian scenes are depicted on calendars, cards and on T-shirts. Indeed, these are the actual scenes you will discover as you travel around our island. For a taste of Carnival, have a look at the Clowns and painted masks.

One Large, Delicious Pizza - coming up fast!
Although better known for its own special Caribbean delicacies, St. Kitts has not neglected that more modern and popular dish - the North American Pizza!

Unique Caribbean Flavours - exported to New York
Located handily, on what is called the Atlantic Strip, at Frigate Bay, you'll find **Paradise Pizza** (Tel: 465-8373) - the home of good pizzas - many with a unique Kittitian twist to their flavour. Several of their many delicious 'specials' have even been 'exported' to New York by returning vacationers and several 're-orders' have been mailed off to various corners of the USA.

Relax in the Covered Courtyard
Paradise Pizza offers an attractive, plant-filled, semi-open courtyard for dining and a very comprehensive menu of modestly priced pizzas. It's not listed on their attractive menu - but do ask about their 'Everything All Together' special - it will keep you busy eating for a long, long time. Naturally, they also have a well stocked bar and an efficient take-out service. Just call ahead to place orders - for your own 'pizza of paradise'.

A tasty pizza in the relaxing semi open-air courtyard of Frigate Bay's popular Paradise Pizza, is a beautiful way to unwind after a busy day of sightseeing.

Photo - Livingston Jackson

Photo - Livingston Jackson

Framed by the leafy boughs of Independence Square's majestic old trees, one finds Duxie's Restaurant, in yet another beautifully preserved historic building.

Dining in a Centuries Old Manor

Originally, a 150-year old Merchant's house, rather than a true Manor, **Duxie's Restaurant** (Tel: 465-2256) is located in a magnificent old, all-wooden building in the top corner of Independence Square - and offers a fine selection of local fare - all lovingly prepared under the personal supervision of 'Duxie' herself.

How to Learn to Pronounce - 'Duxie'

'Duxie' - actually pronounced 'Dooksey', has been the lifelong nickname of Diane Hutchings - who, with her husband David, runs this very popular and successful local Bar and Restaurant. Duxie is a true Kittitian, having been born on the island - and delights in personally hosting this busy town-centre restaurant, both by day and by night.

Specials by Day - Romantic by Night

Apart from a delicious range of daily 'specials' that keep the customers flocking in, Duxie transforms the dining room every night - into a romantic candle-lit 'salon', where one can dine under the original massive wooden ceiling that proudly shows its great ancestry.

A growing number of other restaurants also cater to both tourists and to the local population and many a small spot may well be worth trying out on your visit.

A Town Garden of Delight

The Georgian House on Independence Square is beautifully restored to its original splendour and has a delightful garden. The Patio at Frigate Bay features cooking in the style of the Great Plantation Houses.

Sweet and Sour - to Your Taste

Chinese food fans will find the Sou Tai Restaurant, at Canada Estate, to be the right place. Or down at Conaree Beach, try Jong's Oriental Restaurant & Cisco's Bar for seaside dining.

Real Creole or Curried Conch

Before you leave the island, try JD's on the corner of Church & Princes Streets or sample the generous portions of true Creole dishes at Victor's Hide-Away on Stainforth Street in Basseterre. And J's Place, right at the foot of Brimstone Hill, is just the perfect spot to sample their Curried Conch and local dishes.

Even the busiest visitor enjoys the odd hour of total peace and quiet - and that is something all keen and patient anglers seem to appreciate in abundance.

Photo - Frank Sharman

CHAPTER ELEVEN

Shopping Around - arts, crafts and bargains

Now that you have learned about our history, seen all our beautiful spots and tasted all (or at least some) of our delicious local fruits, vegetables and other foods, it's time to go shopping so you can take home a memento of an unforgettable holiday in our paradise.

Never on a Thursday - except Sometimes

From gemstones to straw baskets, tropical clothing to homemade foods, St. Kitts offers just the souvenir for every taste. Many shops open early and close an hour for lunch. Typical shop hours are 8 a.m. until noon and 1 p.m. until 4 p.m., although variations exist. Thursdays are 'half days' & many shops shut at noon.

E.C. Come - E.C. Go

Banking hours are 8 am until 1 pm, plus Friday afternoons from 3-5 pm. The exchange rate remains steady at between 2.60-2.70 Eastern Caribbean (E.C.) dollars to one US Dollar. Unless otherwise posted, all prices will normally be quoted in EC Dollars - although US Dollars are usually very widely accepted by shops, hotels and taxi drivers alike.

A Bit o' Gossip and a Pound of Mangoes

The Public Market is situated in Irish Town on the Bay Road and it is a "must" visit. Saturday is not only an islander's shopping day but a social one. A quick "chat" and a gossip adds flavour like no other spice.

A Wide and Colourful Variety

For some local villagers, it is a weekly outing and in that way shopping is not a burden but a pleasure. On your visit, you will enjoy seeing the wide and colourful variety of local fish, vegetables and fruit on sale.

Stamps - Courtesy St. Kitts Philatelic Bureau

The beautiful stamps of St. Kitts are eagerly sought by enthusiastic collectors throughout the world - and the local Philatelic Bureau is a popular tourist stop.

With topics ranging from Pirates to Pelicans and Sugarcane to the Christmas Tree Worm - it is not surprising that our colourful postage stamps have fascinated both serious collectors and visitors to our island paradise for many years.

Miniature Works of Art

The ever increasing numbers of tourists and visitors to the country have been quick to realize that the beautiful stamps (they are miniature works of art) make ideal inexpensive souvenirs to take home as reminders of their enjoyable vacations in St. Kitts.

Stamps Ashore, Afloat and Abroad

The St. Kitts Philatelic Bureau, has catered for these discerning clientele in various ways since 1980. Smiling staff greet you when you visit the Bureau's headquarters on Bay Road. More adventurous personnel (just as cheerful!) journey out to the cruise-ships at anchor in the bay, where they put on impromptu displays of St. Kitts' stamps. And an efficient mail-order service is always available - for those who wish to continue their collections.

Undoubtably the most colourful premises in town, the **Caribelle Batik Shop,** is to be found in The Circus.

A Riot of Bright Colours

The beautifully designed batik fashions, all created locally at Romney Manor, feature original Caribbean themes. Caribelle Batik only use the most colourfast dyes and the very finest quality long staple cotton - for their brilliant, rich and vibrantly coloured batik items.

Sailing Up The Wall

Also on display here, are the popular Caribelle Batik Wall Hangings, each featuring unique Caribbean motifs. Palm trees, majestic windmills, exotic hibiscus and other tropical flowers, sailing ships - these splendid works of art are superb reminders of life in paradise.

A Difficult Choice

Caribelle's helpful staff are always happy to guide you through the vast choice of original batik - T-shirts, shorts, beach wraps, dresses and swimwear, all are available in a variety of sizes. The beautiful colours and tempting designs often make your choice difficult.

Brightly coloured, casually-cut Caribelle Batik fashions are snapped up by visitors as reminders of the romantic and relaxing atmosphere of tropical island living.

Photo - Caribelle Batik

Photo. - Livingston Jackson

A Treasure Trove of Duty-Free Delights- is how a recent visitor described the vast selection of perfumes, jewellery and gifts at A Slice of the Lemon's busy shop.

The way to a woman's heart? The answer is simple: perfumes, gold and diamonds - and all the other 'simple' things in life. All that and more is available at Fort Street's **A Slice of the Lemon** Duty Free shop.

Direct from France - and Duty Free!
Here you will find the island's largest selection of perfumes, toilet waters, colognes and aftershaves, mostly direct from France and all at very low duty-free prices. And always 'specials' - offering extra savings!

Save Yourself 50%
Exquisite Dartington & Sevres crystal and fine china, such as Goebel, Portmeirion and Coalport, can be bought from A Slice of the Lemon - at 50% off prices normally found in North America.

Affordable Luxury and Tempting Value
This spacious shop, with its vast array of 'treasures', features fine, as well as costume jewellery in unique designs and famous watches - all carefully selected from around the world. Visit A Slice of the Lemon and be guided to affordable luxury by their caring staff.

A Caribbean compendium, **PalmCrafts** offers the best from around the islands. Take a bit of Kittitian flavour back home, with locally made jams, jellies and chutneys from their Kittitian Kitchen. Sunny Caribbee aromatic spice bundles make inexpensive gifts that can be enjoyed with more than one sense. And, if your vacation has been heavy on rum punches, pick up one of PalmCraft's local herb tea remedies for 'hangovers'.

Catch a Live Wooden Fish

Located in the Palms Arcade, PalmCrafts also has a lovely array of hand-made clothing from Southern Cross and Caribee Clothes in Nevis, hand-screened fabrics from Cinnamon Hill - plus larimar, coconut and amber jewellery. A very popular PalmCrafts item is the brightly painted and carved wooden fishes, all so accurate as to look alive.

Postcards and Potions

PalmCrafts also has a wide assortment of exotic fragrances, skin lotions and bath oils. And a selection of local colour postcards, PalmCrafts certainly takes some beating for sheer choice.

The fascinating PalmCrafts shop is just the place to browse and discover the perfect gift or souvenir to remind you of your unforgettable vacation.

Photo - Livingston Jackson

There comes a time on all vacations, when one needs a little extra cash - and visitors with Traveller's Cheques to cash, usually find their way to **The Royal Bank of Canada**'s handy premises at the Circus.

Beauty and Brightness Combined

Although one of the island's oldest established Banks, with the usual full range of modern banking services - the Royal Bank's claim to local fame and banking leadership in St. Kitts, (as reputed by many Kittitians), stems from the fact the Royal have apparently snapped up most of the island's brightest and prettiest girls.

Front Line Efficiency and Charm

Tellers are a bank's 'front line' - the smiling faces that greet the customers every day - and the Royal's efficient staff make banking a distinct pleasure. No doubt the Royal's appointment of the island's first lady Assistant Bank Manager - has much to do with it.

Other banks include Barclays, Bank of Nova Scotia, the National Bank and the island's own Development Bank - plus the Central Bank for the Eastern Caribbean.

The imposing 19th Century style premises of the centrally located Royal Bank of Canada, house an efficient & modern, computerised international banking system.

Photo - Livingston Jackson

Photo - Livingston Jackson

The Shoreline Plaza, beside the town centre's Treasury, is home to several small souvenir, gift and craft shops - and features a waterfront bar and local restaurant.

The **Shoreline Plaza,** by The Treasury on Bay Road, is a 'one-stop' shopping centre which offers a range of 'duty free' gifts, souvenirs & island crafts, plus fine local food - all in one handy and relaxing spot.
Among the neat little shops in the Plaza, one will find **TropiCrafts**, which offers visitors a dazzling selection of high quality gifts in leather, china and glass, to tempt all tastes. Right opposite, you will also find the sweet-smelling premises of **Sensational**, where a new world of exotic scents, fine jewellery and sensational gifts is neatly laid out before your eyes. And just a few steps away, the fascinating shelves of **La Poinciana**, which house a beautiful array of hand-crafted wood carvings, shell and coral jewellery, plus the widest range of embroidered linens on the island.

'The Eye-Catching Centre of Handicrafts' - is how the **Emporium de Craft** styles its spacious display, where the skill of our local Craftsmen is displayed - in souvenirs and gifts, all made from local materials.
After shopping around the Plaza - stop and relax over a refreshing cold drink or some fine local cuisine at **QT's Delight Waterfront Bar & Restaurant**.

A Spacious Plaza to take a stroll through
Interlinking the busy department store of TDC, the island's largest conglomerate, is their spacious new **TDC Shopping Plaza,** handily located right in the heart of down-town Basseterre's main shopping area, which is mainly located around Fort Street.

A Courtyard, Fountain and a Coffeeshop
Home to an good selection of shops, the TDC Plaza offers a relaxing stroll, as you wander through the courtyard, past the sparkling fountain, to browse through the jewellery choices displayed at **Objects of Art**, select some menswear at the **Casanova** boutique, visit **TDC's Duty Free Shop** or the **TDC Nick-Nacks** giftshop and explore the **Gold Plus** jewellery store.

Two Spoonful's of Dollars or just One?
Tarry awhile, to inspect your finds at the Plaza's relaxing Restaurant or the **Rose Bud Coffeeshop**, before you pop into the handy branch of **The Bank of Nova Scotia** to change a few Traveller's Cheques, in order to snap up a couple more bargains from the large range of gifts & goodies on offer at TDC Plaza.

An innovatively designed courtyard featuring a water fountain, is the centrepiece that attracts strolling visitors to the TDC Shopping Plaza, on downtown Fort Street.

Photo - Livingston Jackson

Beside the Caribbean beach, the Craftshouse seeks to afford training and employment to allow local craftsmen to develop their own natural skills and talents.

See the Craftsmen At Work
On the edge of the town, a short walk from the Circus, just out along the Bay Road - you will find a fascinating spot, where you may see skilled Kittitian craftsmen at work, making a variety of the island's local souvenirs you will also see on sale in many of the town's shops.

Parker's province - teaching the new skills
Presided over by Ellis Parker, the energetic manager of this government-supported enterprise, **The Craftshouse** offers local craft entrepreneurs a base from which to work - and a chance to learn new skills in crafts production, using the Craftshouse's many handy facilities and Parker's marketing advice.

Visit the 'Factory' Shop
Attached to the Craftshouse is a small shop, where many of the wares produced by local islanders are on display and for sale - all at very reasonable prices. The profits from these sales are split between the artisans and the Craftshouse. An increasing number of the local craftsmen are now beginning to use this modern and comprehensive facilities as their personal 'factory'.

Drop a Line to the Folks at Home
The Post Office, on Bay Road, is open from 8 am until 3 pm daily, except Thursdays when it closes at 11 am.

Bare Necessities - Food and Medicines
Two of St. Kitts largest supermarkets, **Ram's** and the **Scotch House**, are located, on the Bayfront, opposite Shoreline Plaza. Other markets **Cemaco, Eskimo Foods** and **B & K** - whilst **Skerrit's Drug Store, City Drug Store** & **Medic's Pharmacy** offer prescriptions.

Smile Please - Ready in an Hour
If you can't wait to see your photographs, **Quick Photo Labs** on the Frigate Bay Road will process them fast!

Instant Copies and Quick Printing - with a smile!
The best source for reading material, **Wall's Bookstore** on Fort Street, also has a Record and Tape section. Apart from books, they offer the island's largest range of Colour Postcards, published by St. Kitts' leading printers and designers, the **Creole Graphics Printery & Publishing Studio** - who operate an efficient Quick Print and busy Photocopying service in Liverpool Row.

This popular hairstyle, reflecting the islander's Afro-Caribbean roots is often requested by fashion conscious visitors to the island's many hairstylists.

Photo - Livingston Jackson

CHAPTER TWELVE

Sports and Activities - the gentle diversions

Sports play a major part in the lives of the people of St. Kitts. Not only are Cricket and Football played extensively, but Netball, Boxing and Athletics also attract substantial followings.

Cricket, Cricket... lovely Cricket

Cricket is the national sport of St. Kitts, being played by all boys from an early age. As you pass through the island's towns and villages you will often see the game being played at all levels by young and old alike. All you need is a short plank of wood as a crude bat, three sticks to make the stumps, a ball and a small open area and you have all the ingredients for an island Cricket game. The island boasts many Cricket clubs who compete against each other in the SKANTEL Leagues and St. Kitts always fields a strong local team in the Leeward Islands Cricket Championships. St. Kitts won the Nissan Leeward Islands Trophy in 1986.

Jump and Shoot!

When the young men of St. Kitts play Cricket, the ladies play Netball. The game was introduced into the island some 50 years ago and has been played seriously ever since. Netball reached a peak in the 1970's, when the St. Kitts team became the West Indies Champions on two occasions.

Ask for a Middleweight Rum Punch

St. Kitts has produced several boxers over the years; names such as Easy Boy Ken and Fancy Boy Junior. Roy Gumbs, the 1983 Commonwealth Middleweight Champion, has now hung up his gloves and returned home to run the popular Kittitian Monkey Beach Bar and Watersports at Frigate Bay's Caribbean beach.

Kicking Real Leather
Next to Cricket, Football (Soccer) is the most popular island sport and played throughout the island. Some 33 teams compete annually in the Carib Leagues.

Seriously Working Out
Take a stroll early in the morning or evening and wherever you go you will see Joggers, Runners and Cyclists seriously working out.

All at Sea
The St. Kitts and Nevis Sailing Regatta is a yearly event in which two categories of craft take part; Sailfish and Windsurfers. The course finishes at Oualie Beach, where the celebrations last well into the night.

Fore, Nine or Eighteen?
St. Kitts has two golf courses, the International Championship 18-hole Royal St. Kitts course at Frigate Bay and the 9-hole Golden Rock course near to the airport. The Royal St. Kitts course stretches between the Caribbean and the Atlantic Ocean, where one can enjoy a high quality 18 holes and superb scenery.

Apart from the warmth, watersports in the calm Caribbean waters are undoubtedly one of the leading attractions to visitors coming in from the colder northern climes.

Photo - Frank Sharman